Patterns coloring book

Volume 2

by Dalu

Copyright ©2021 by Dalu
All rights reserved

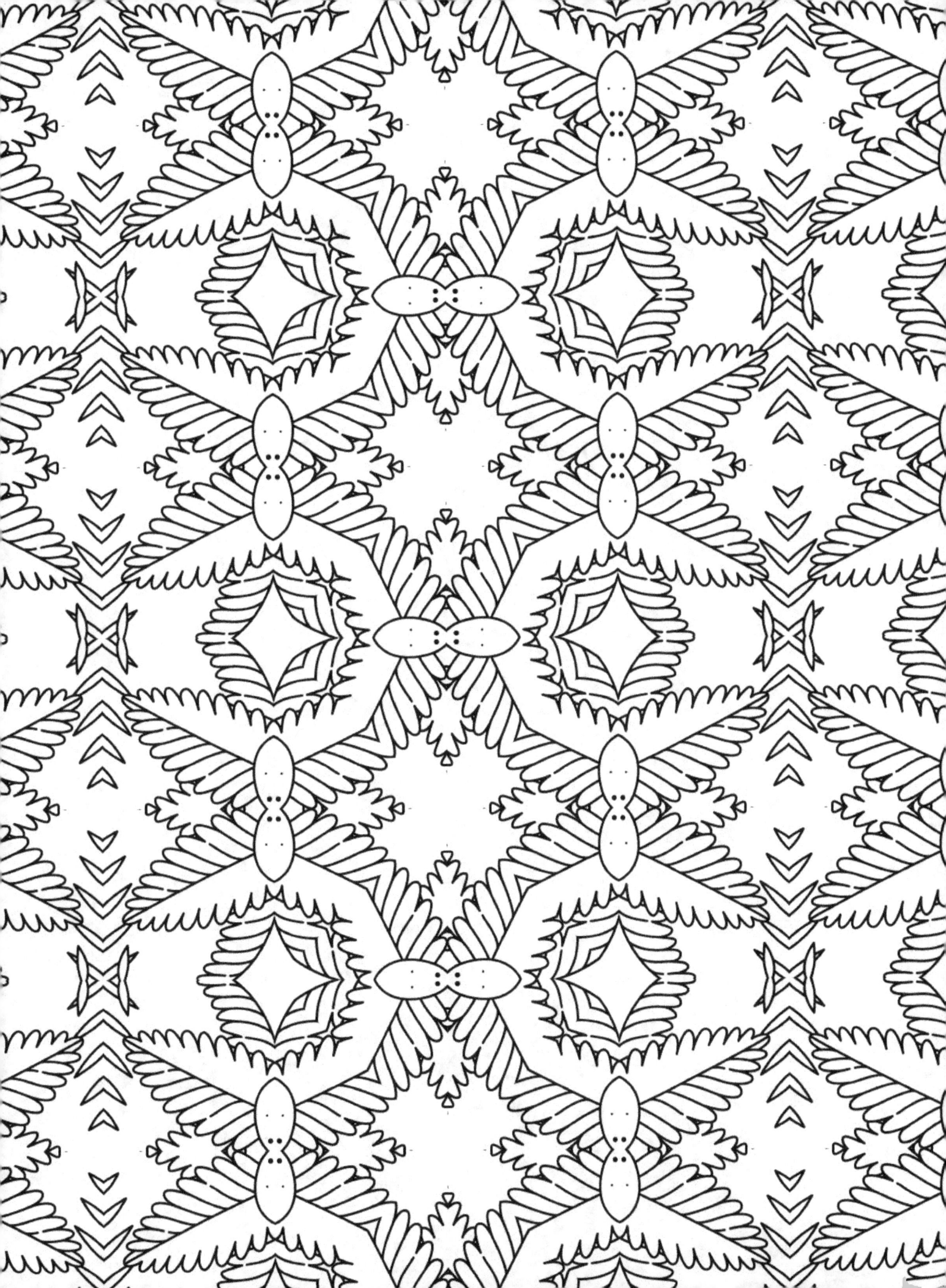

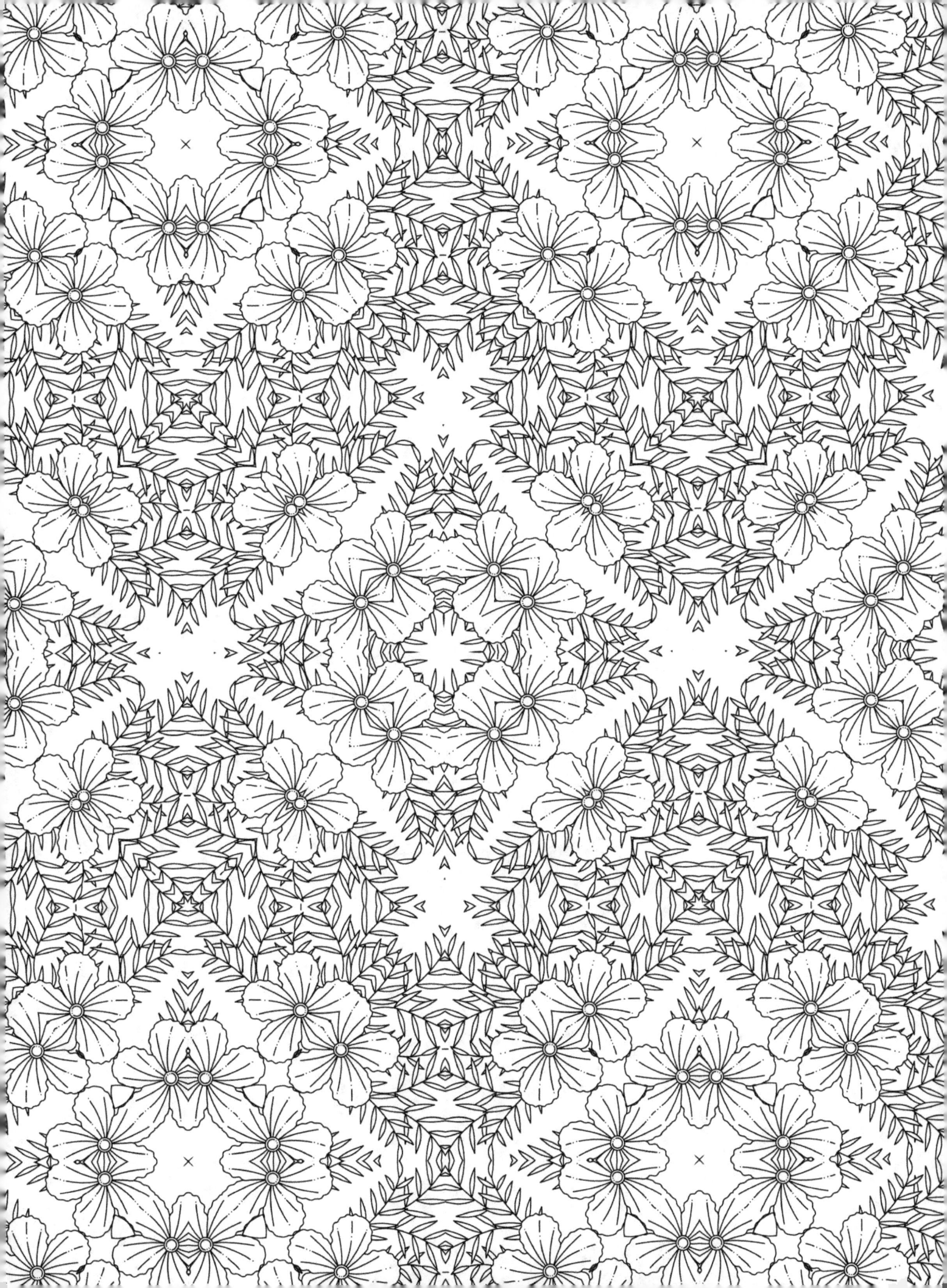

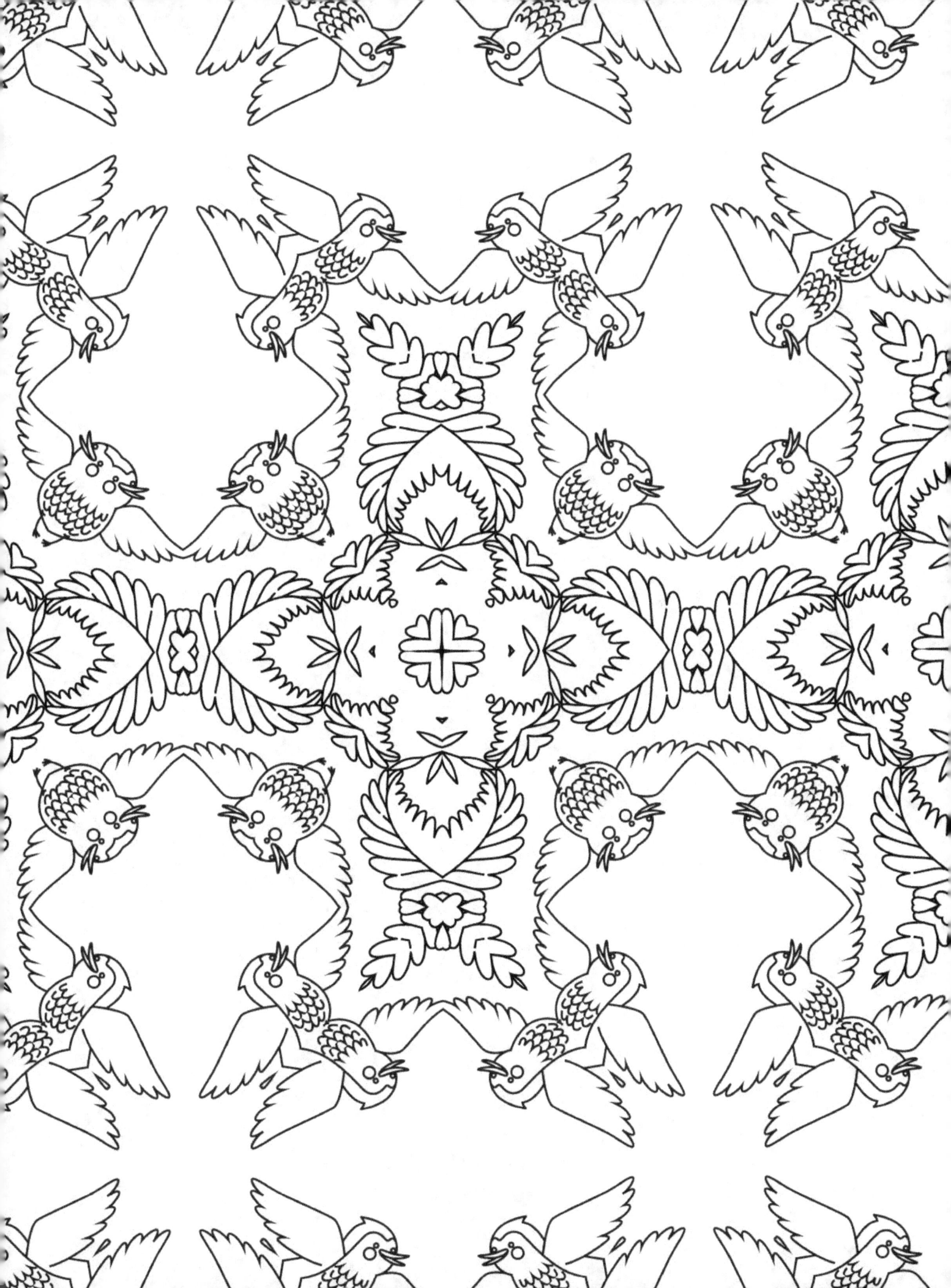

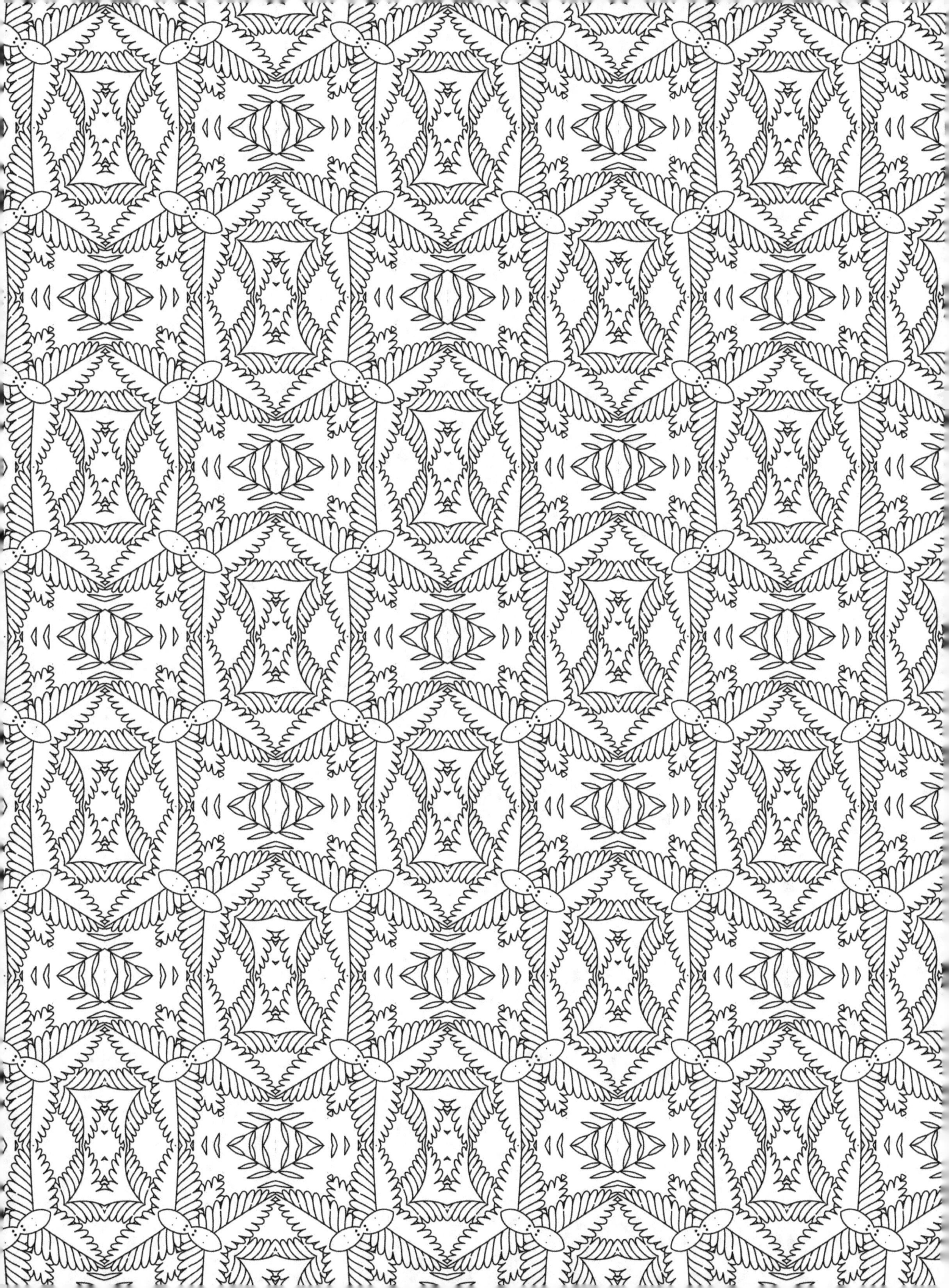

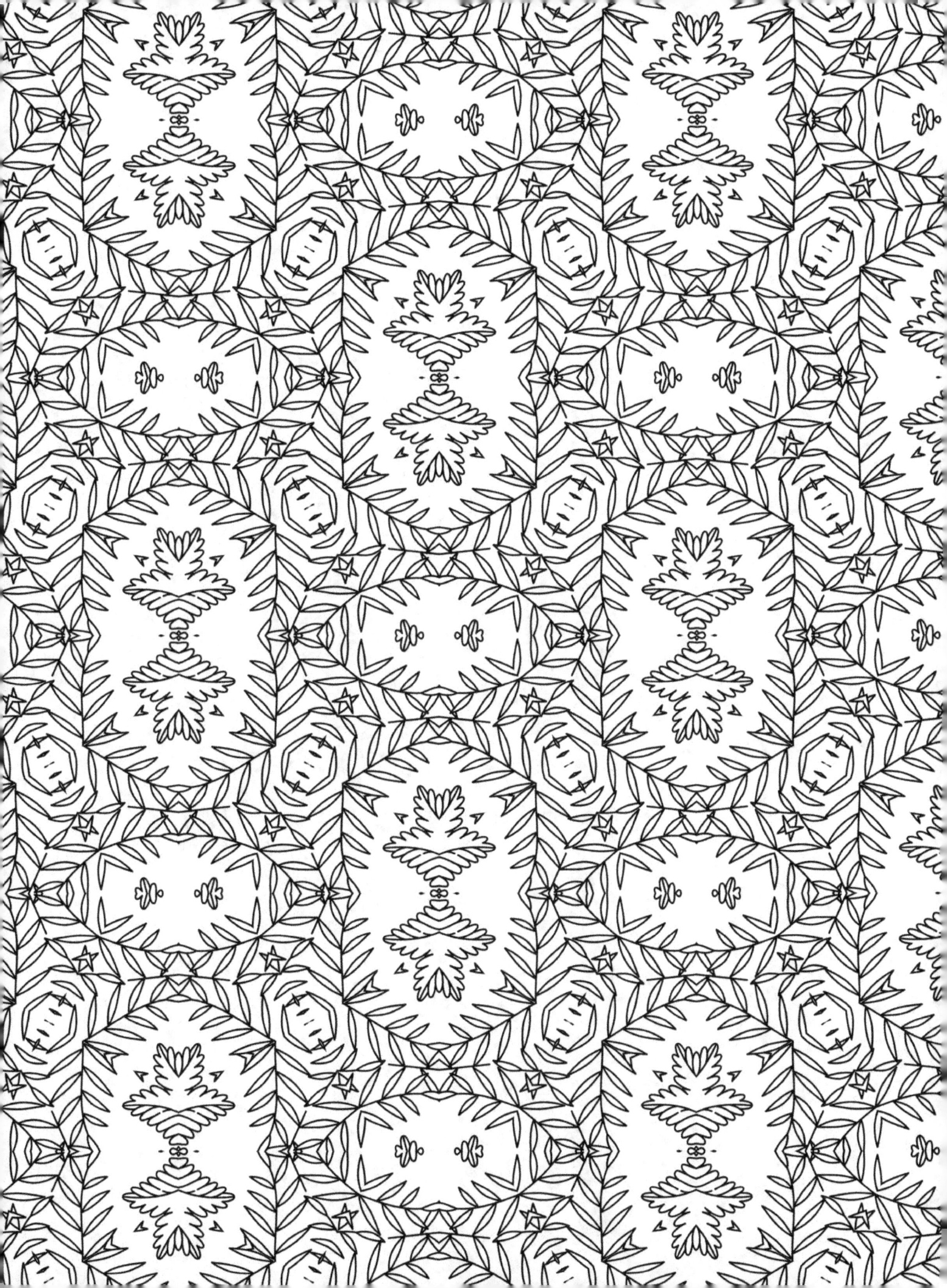

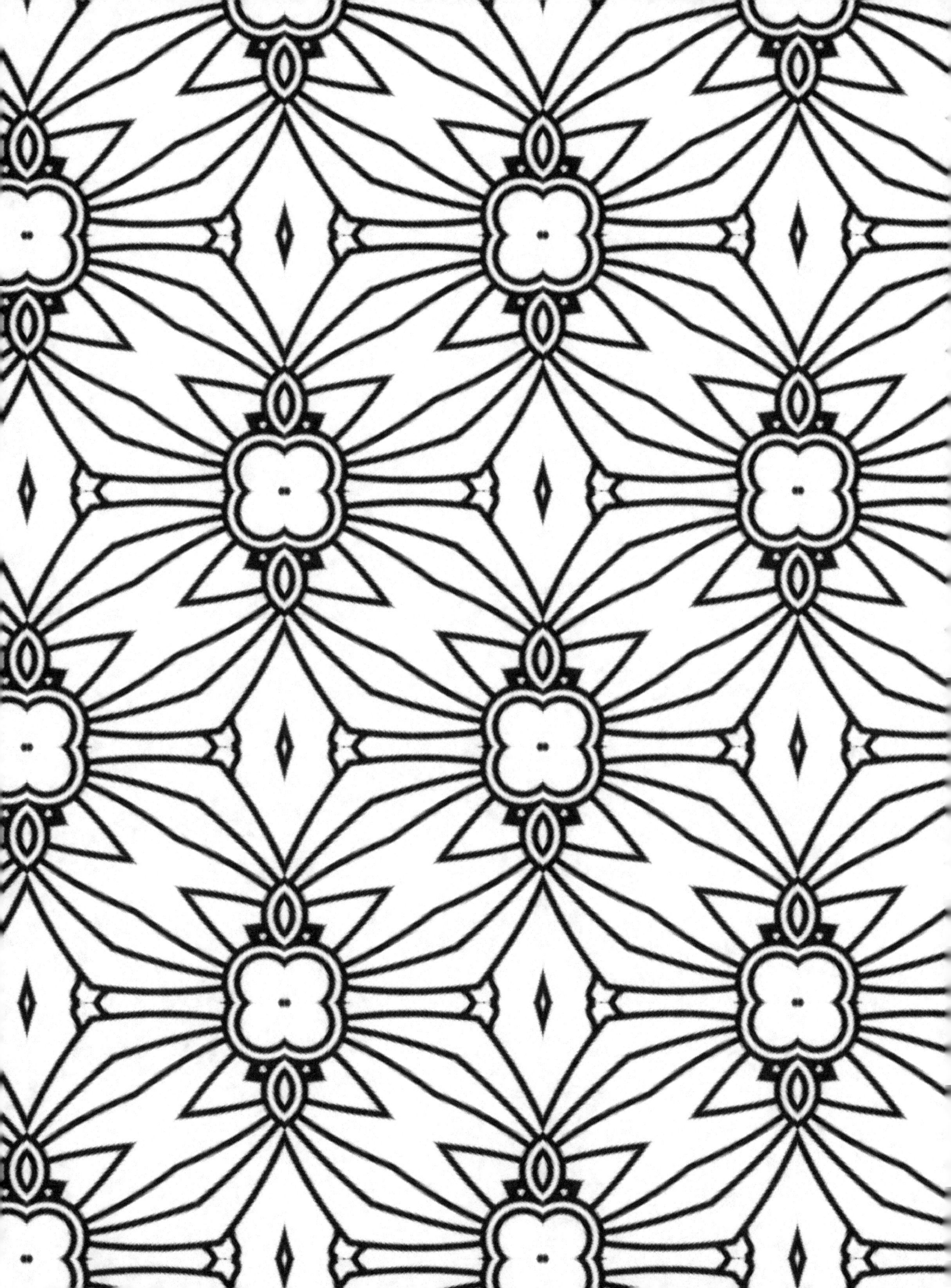

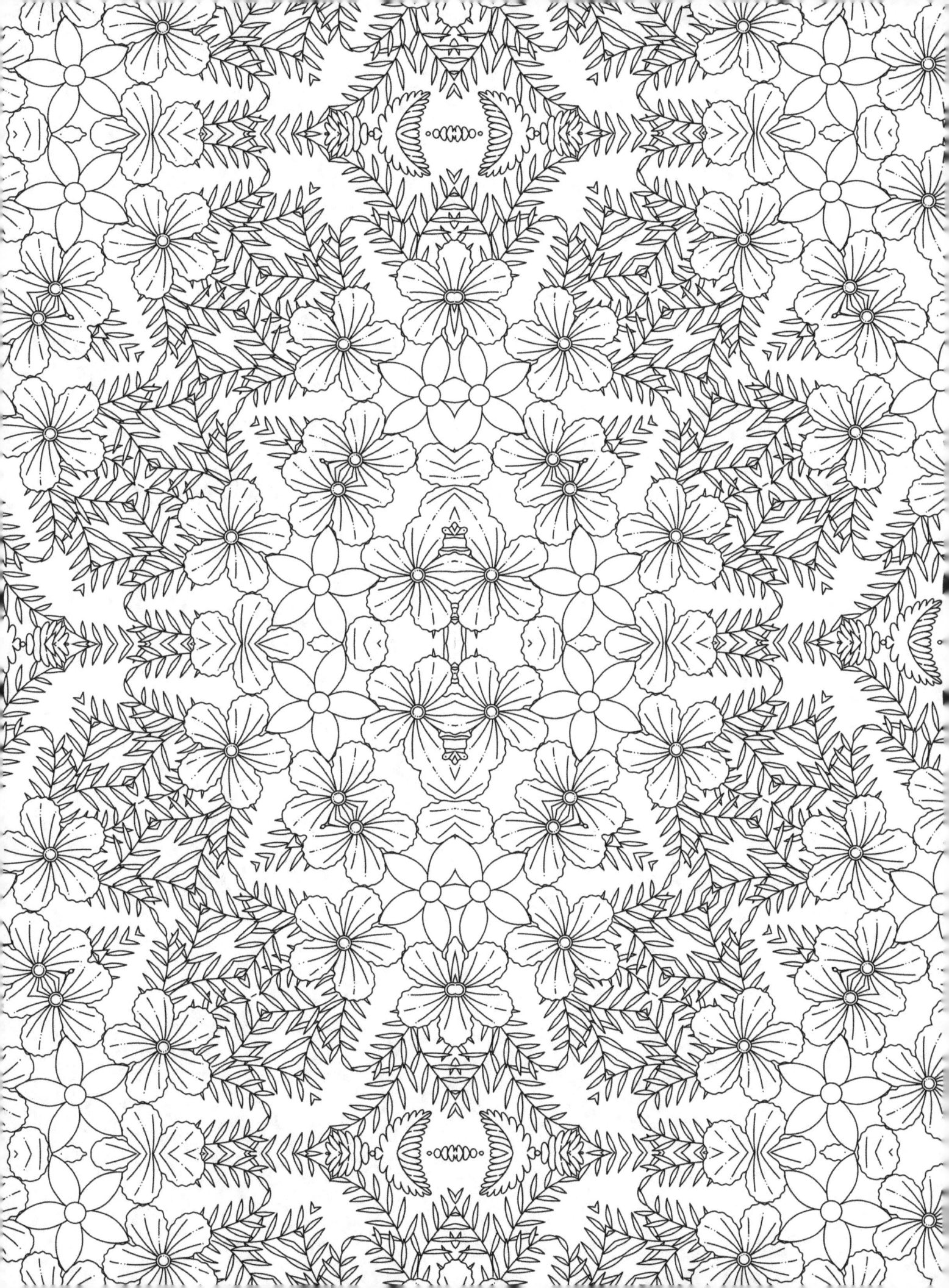

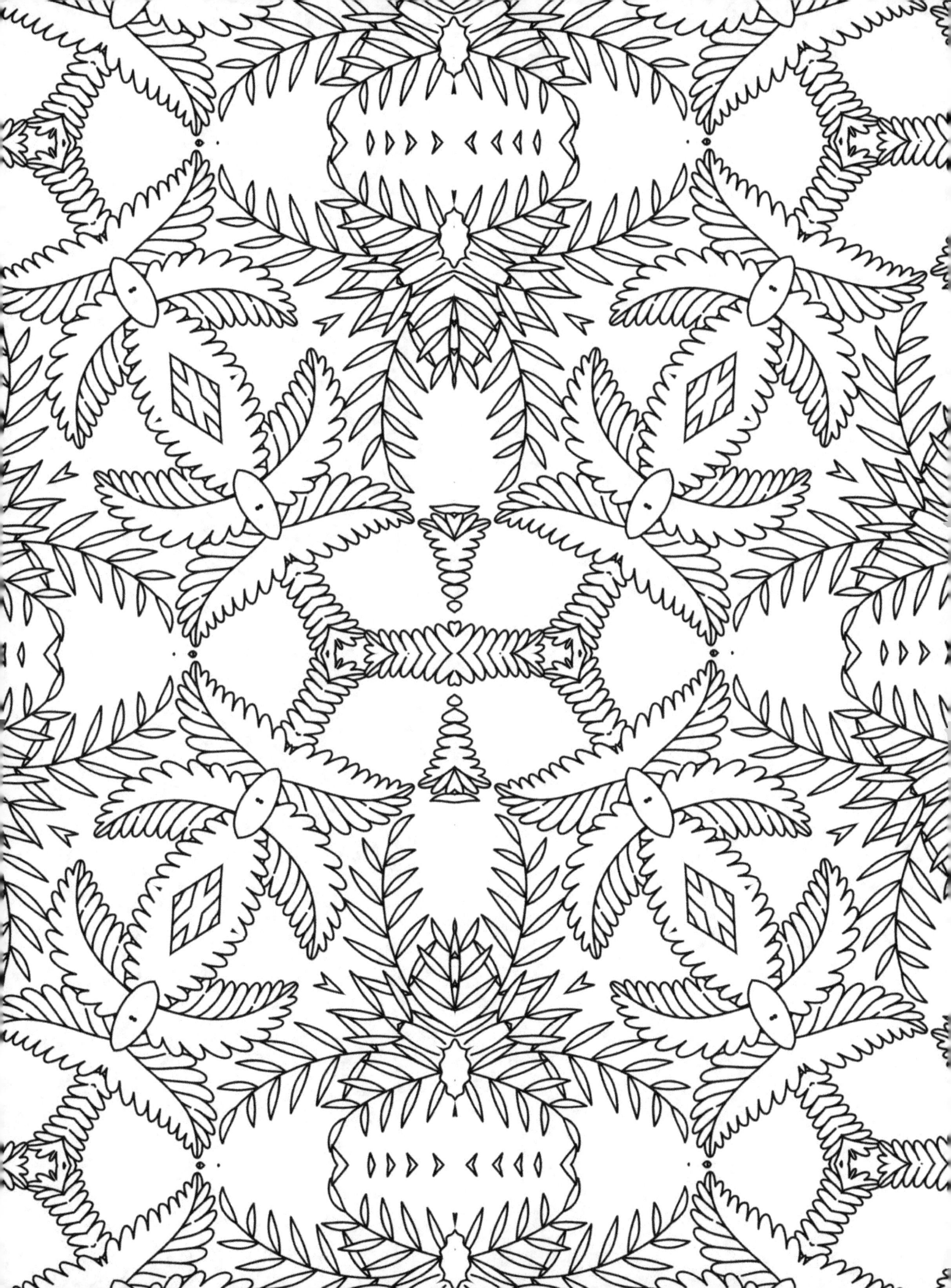

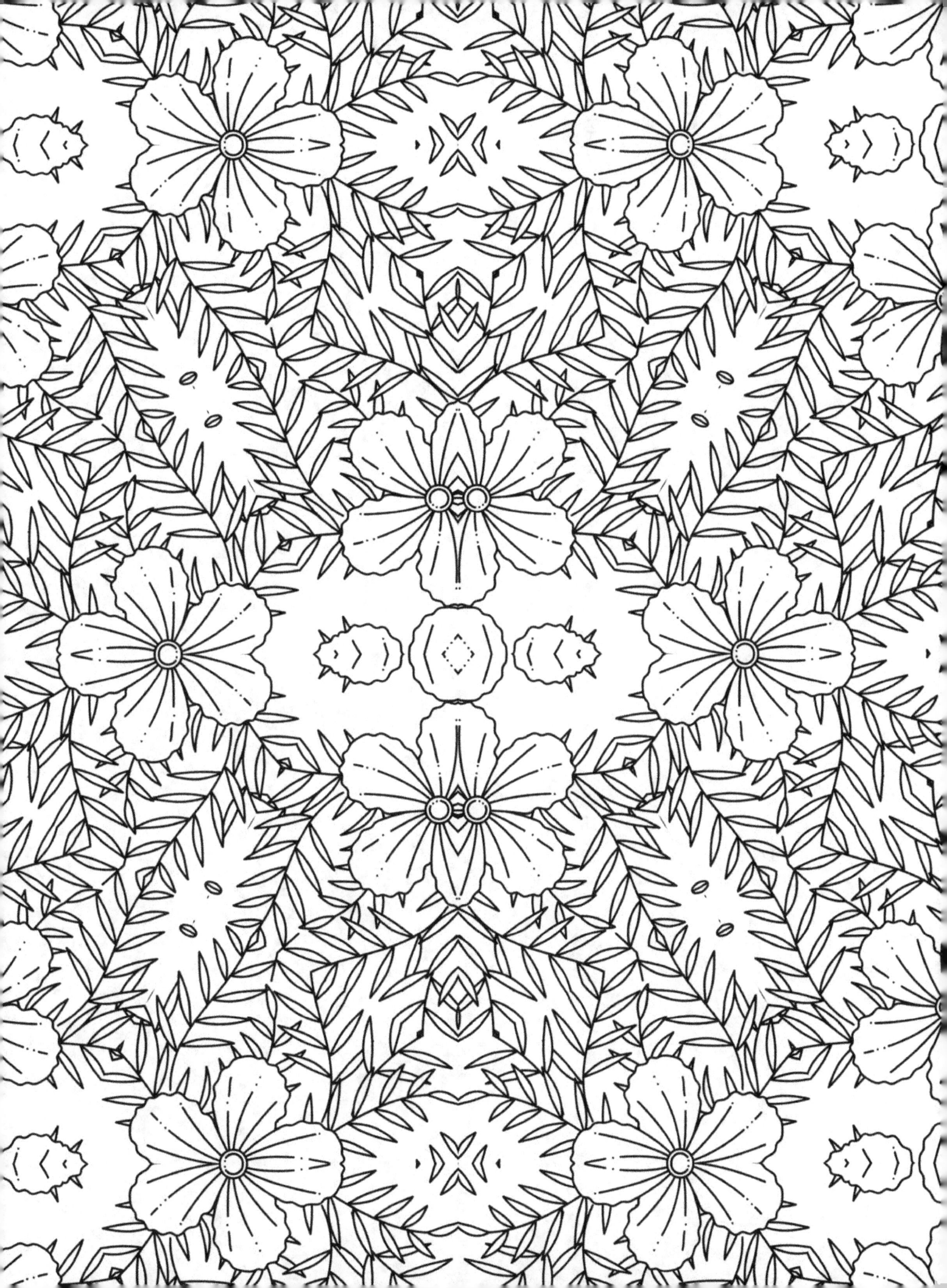

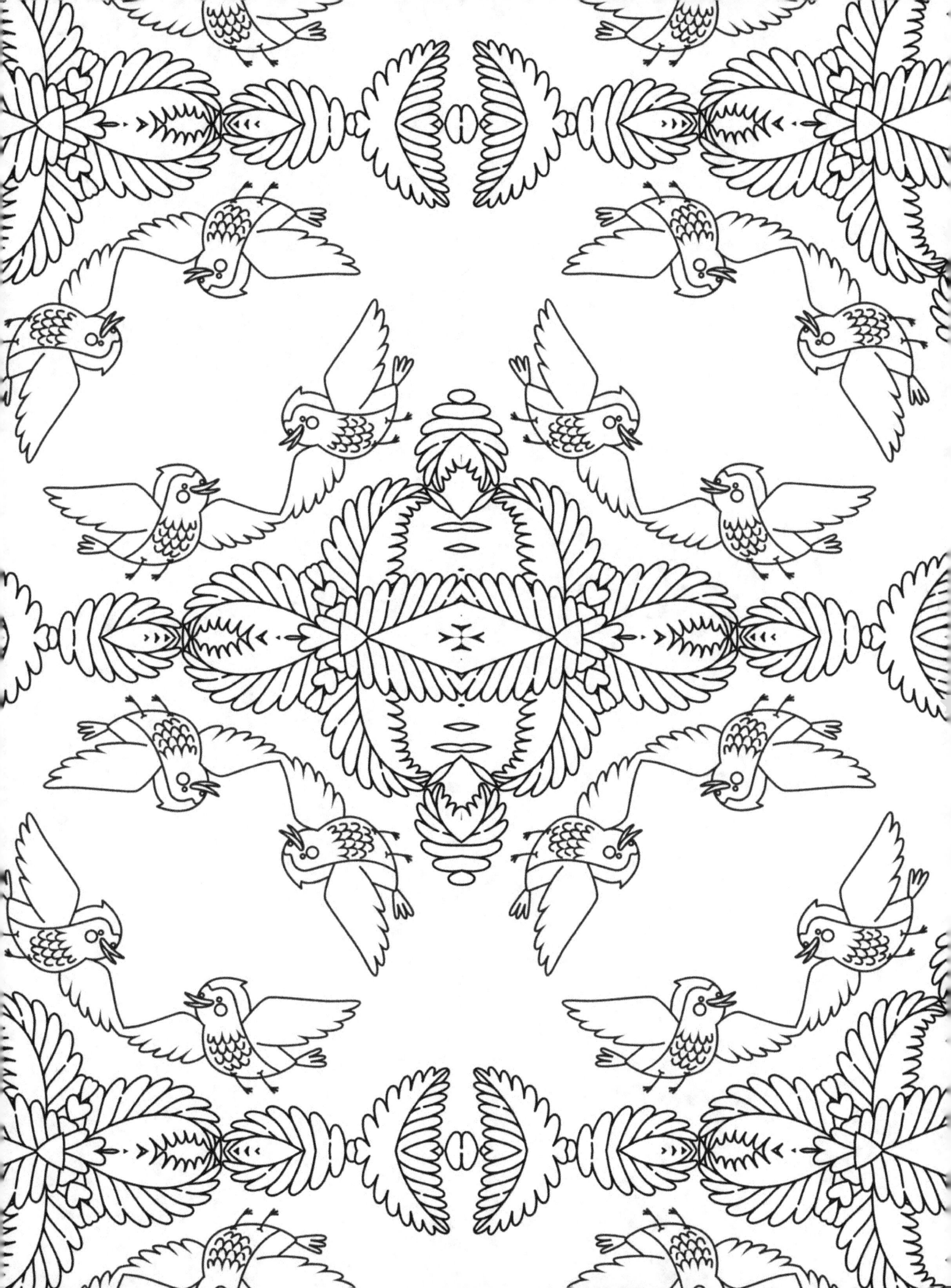

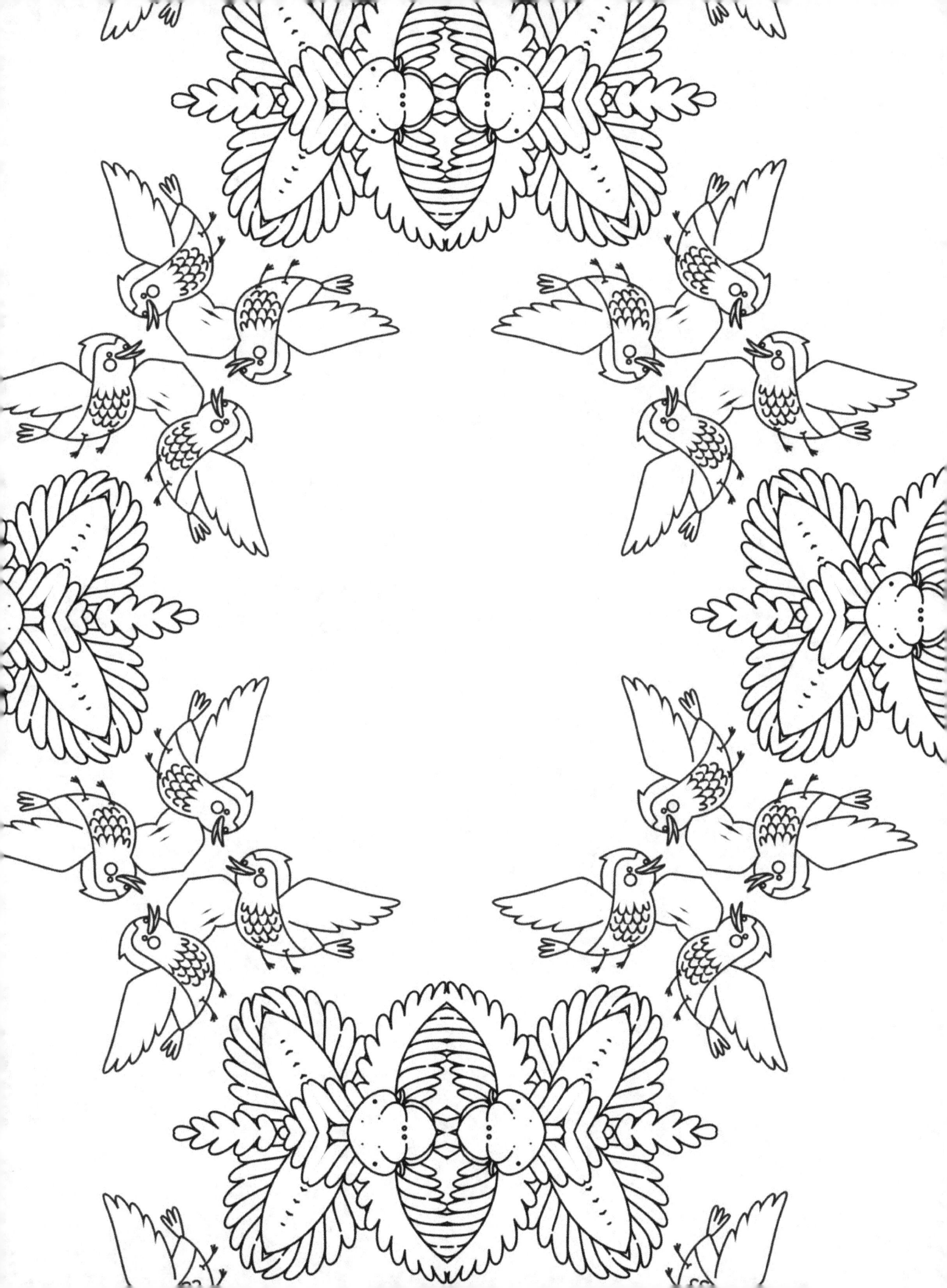

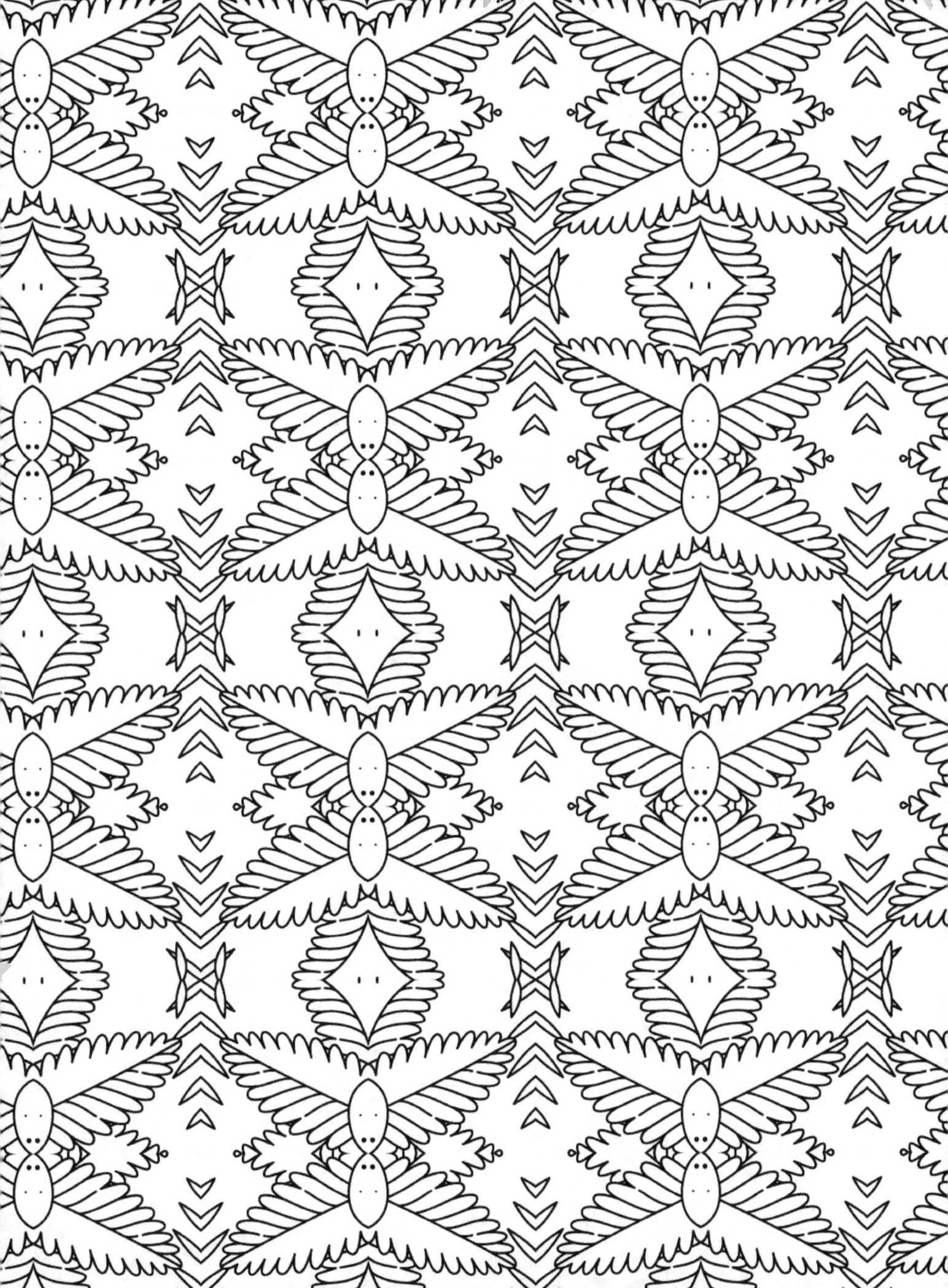

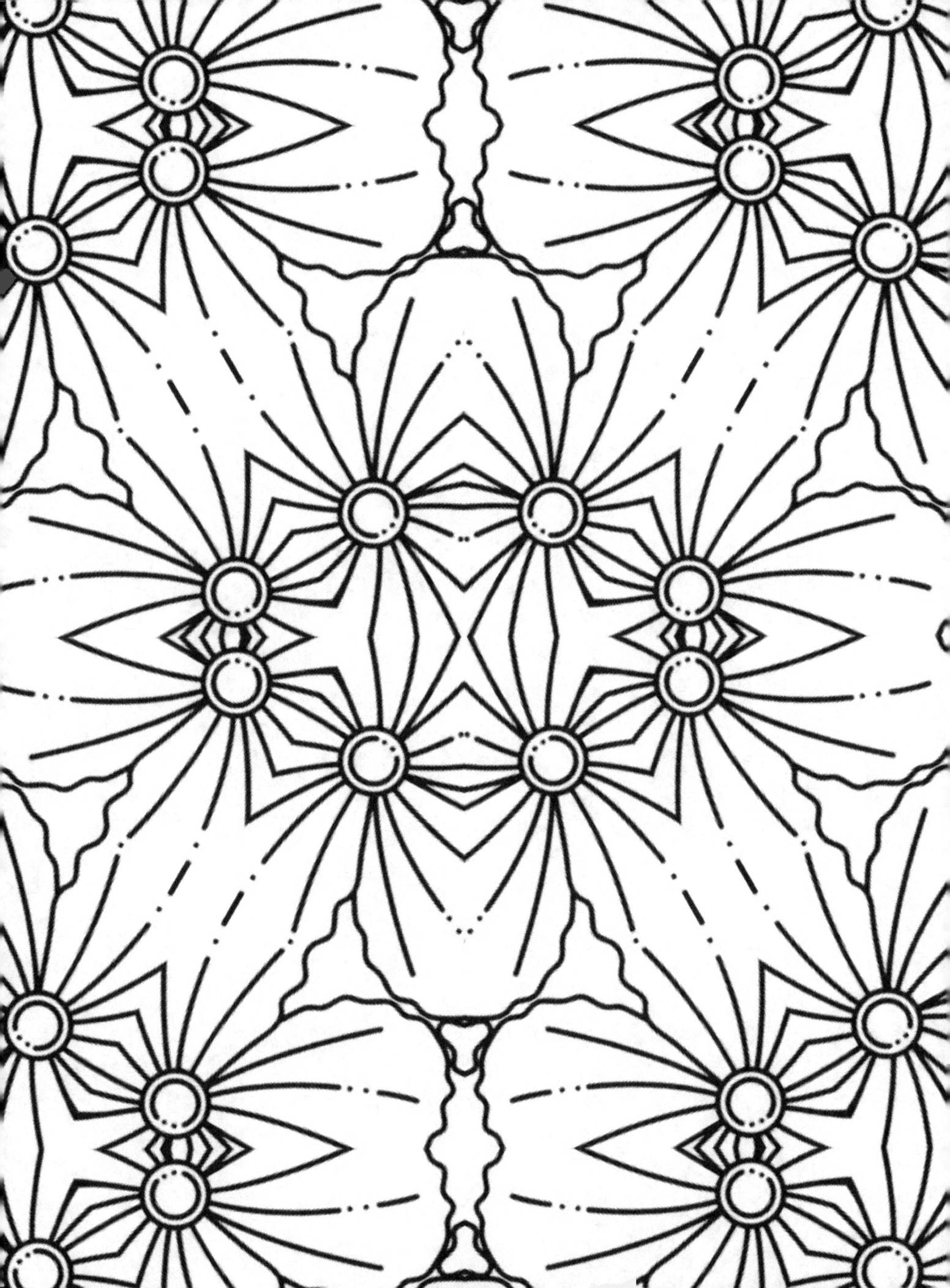

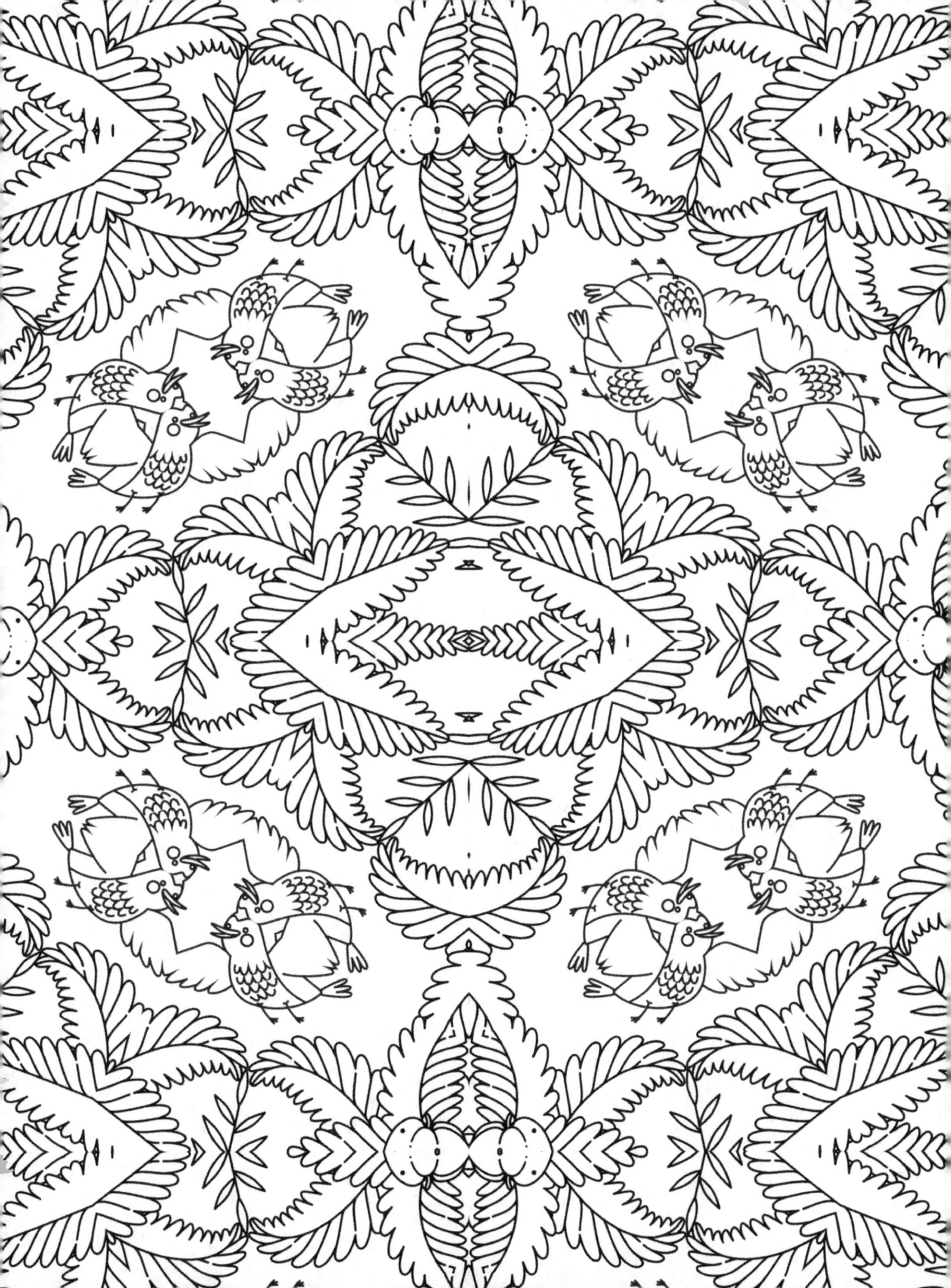

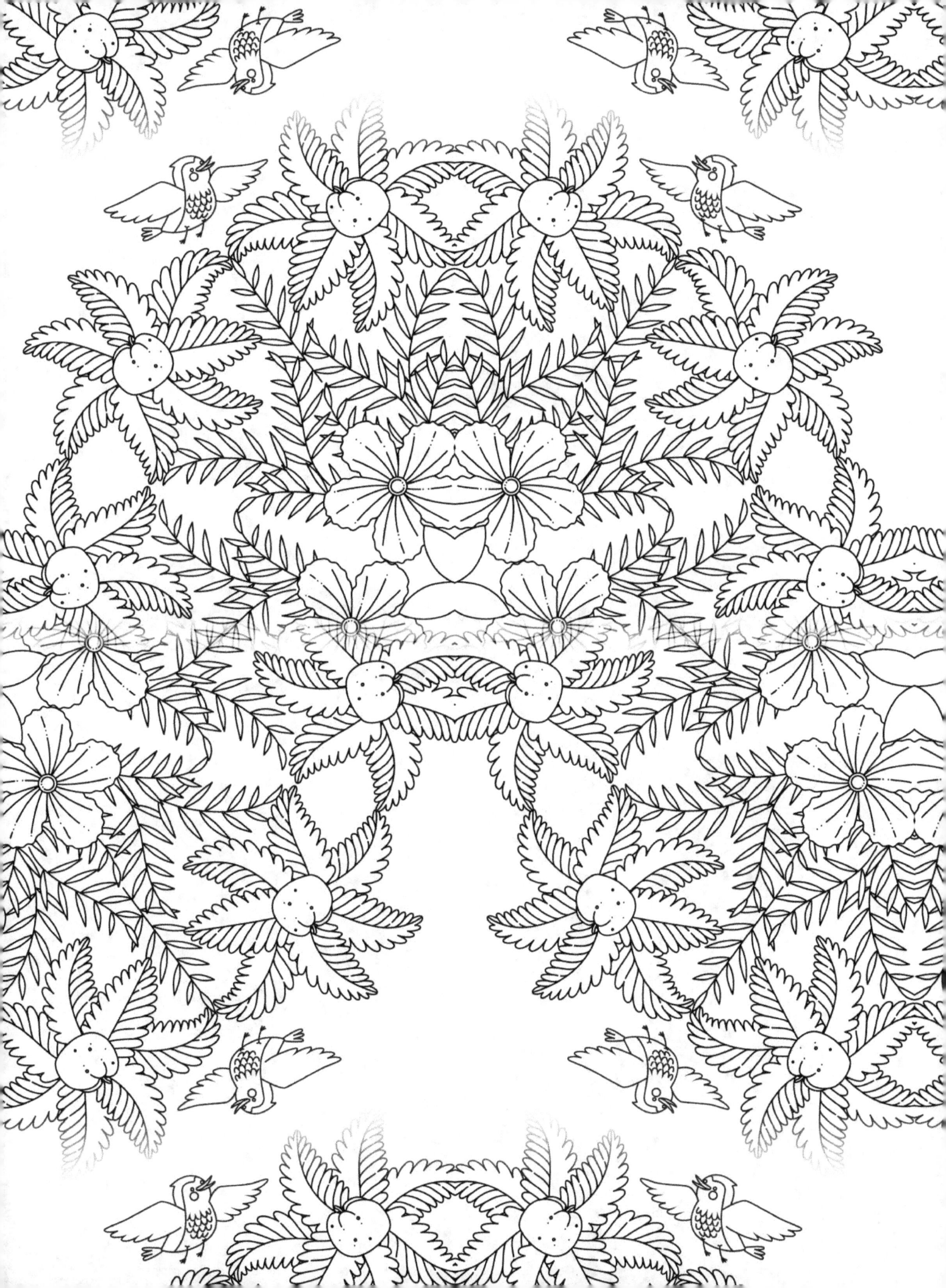

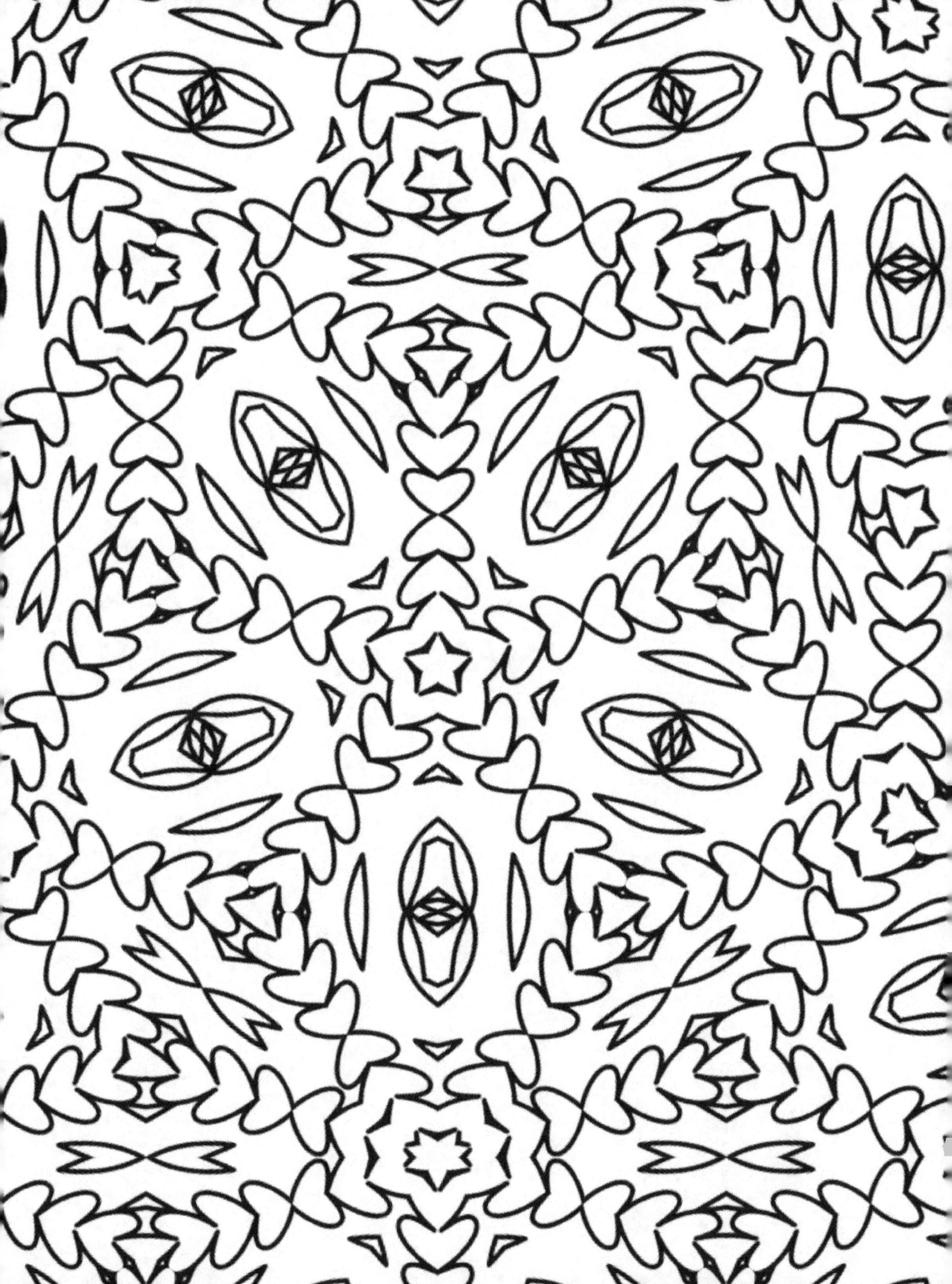

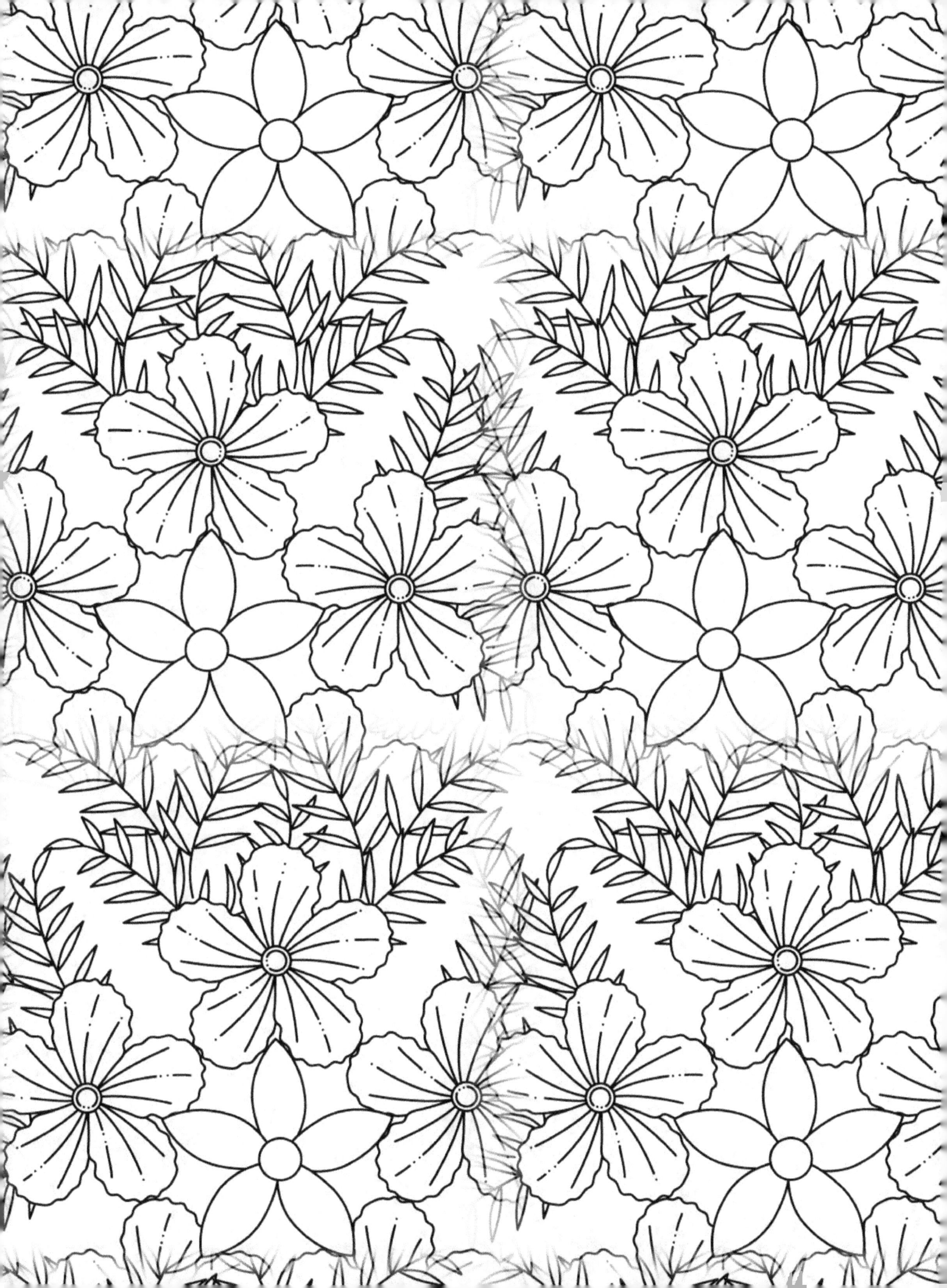

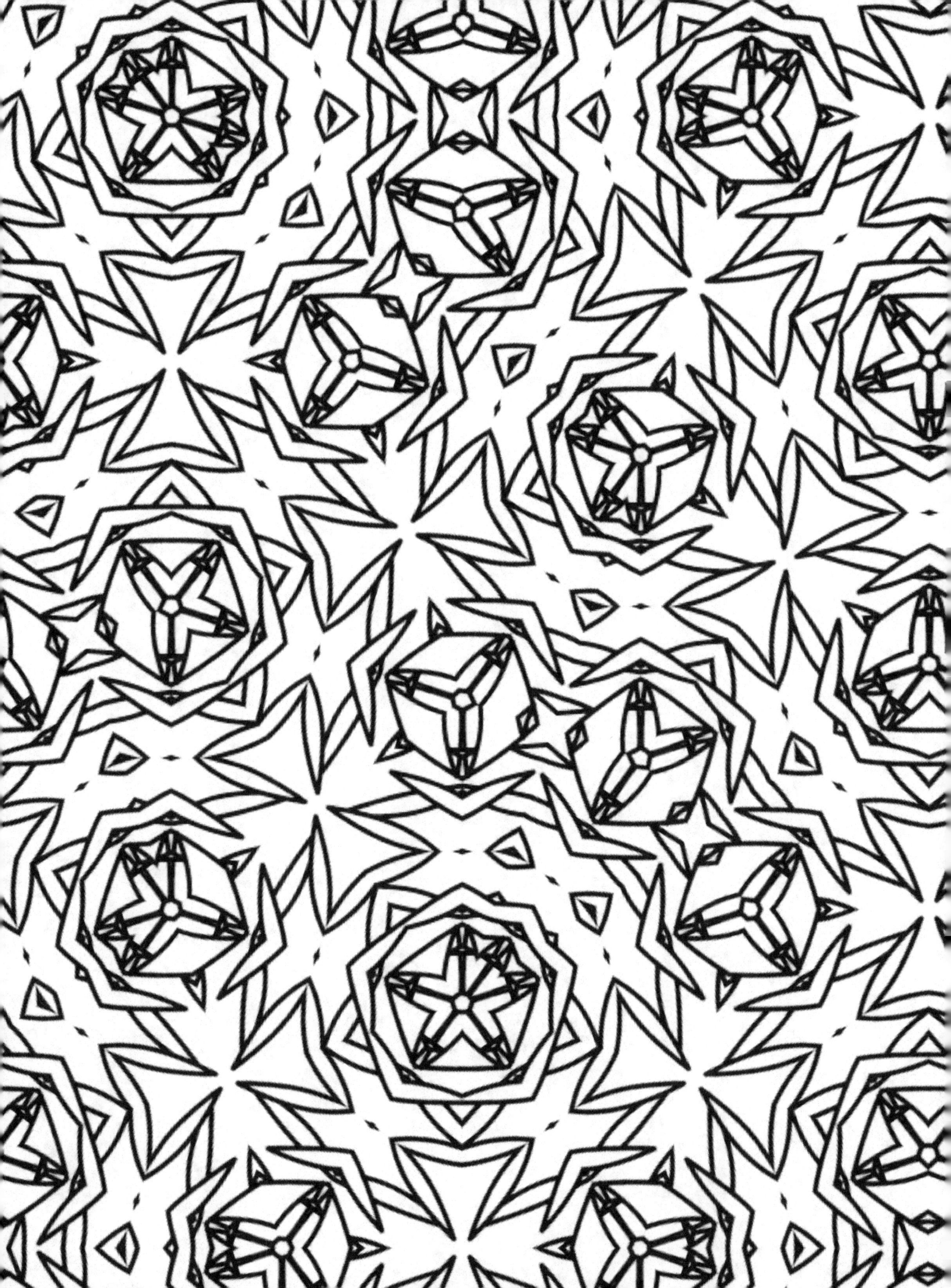

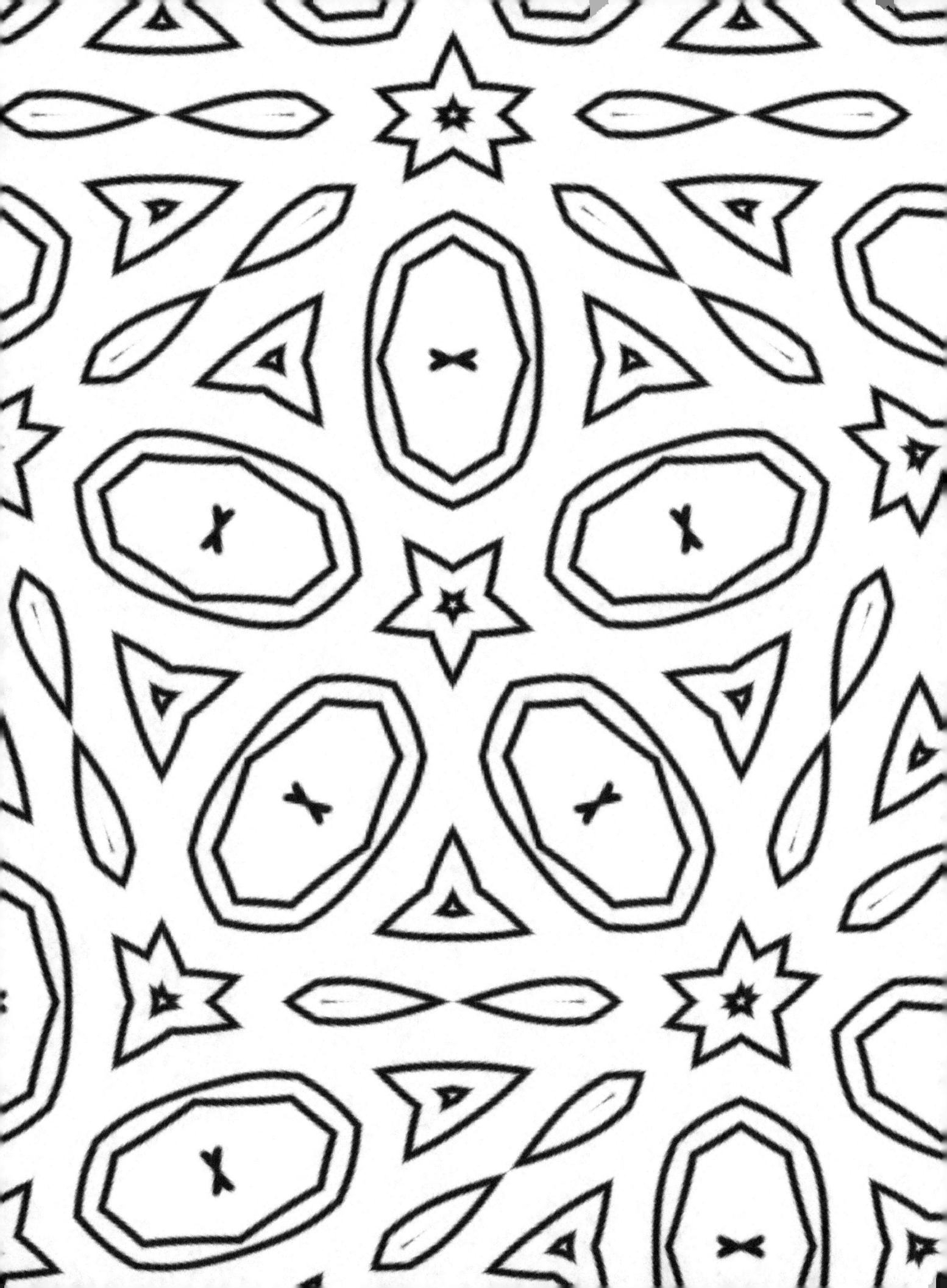

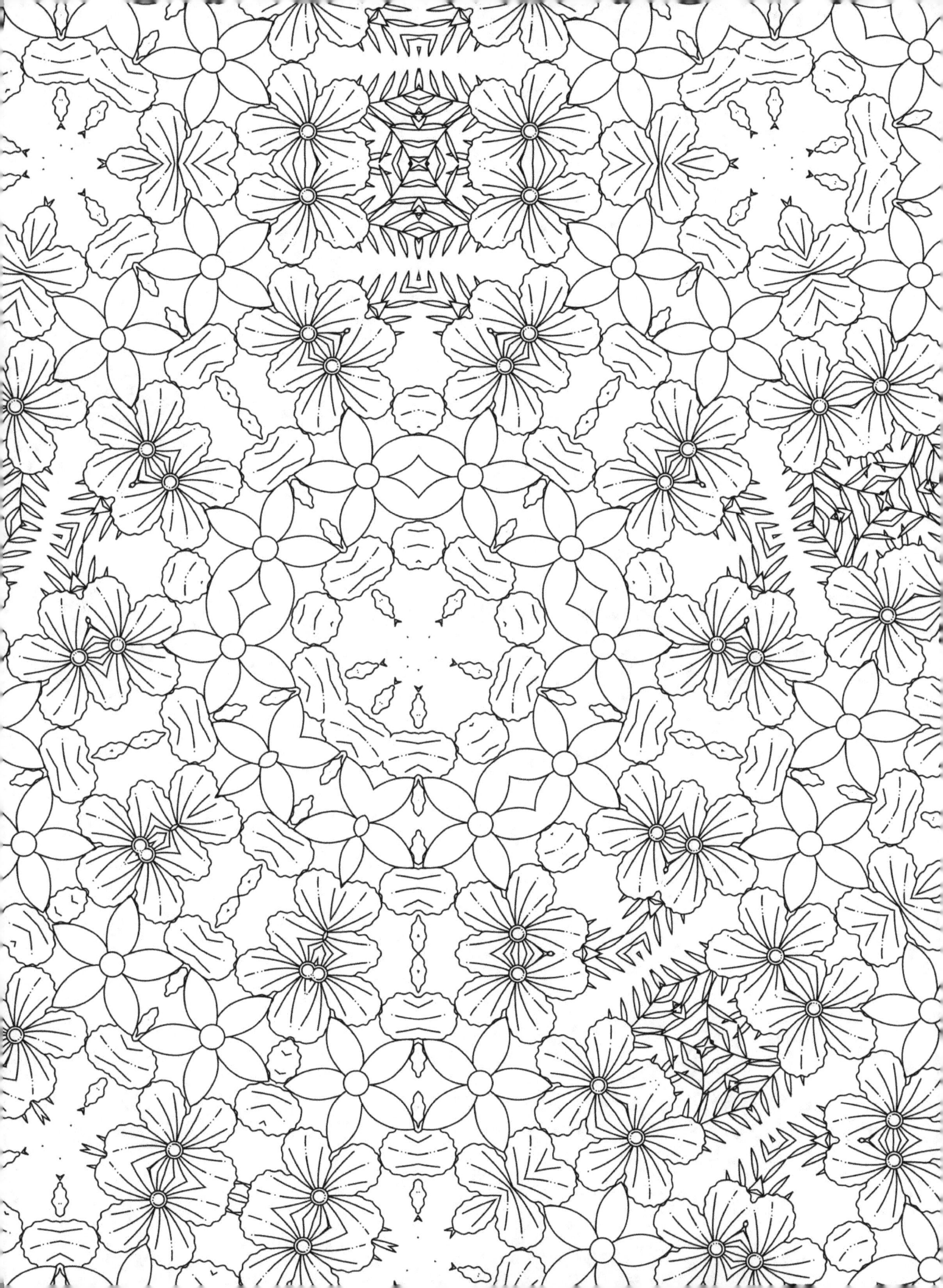

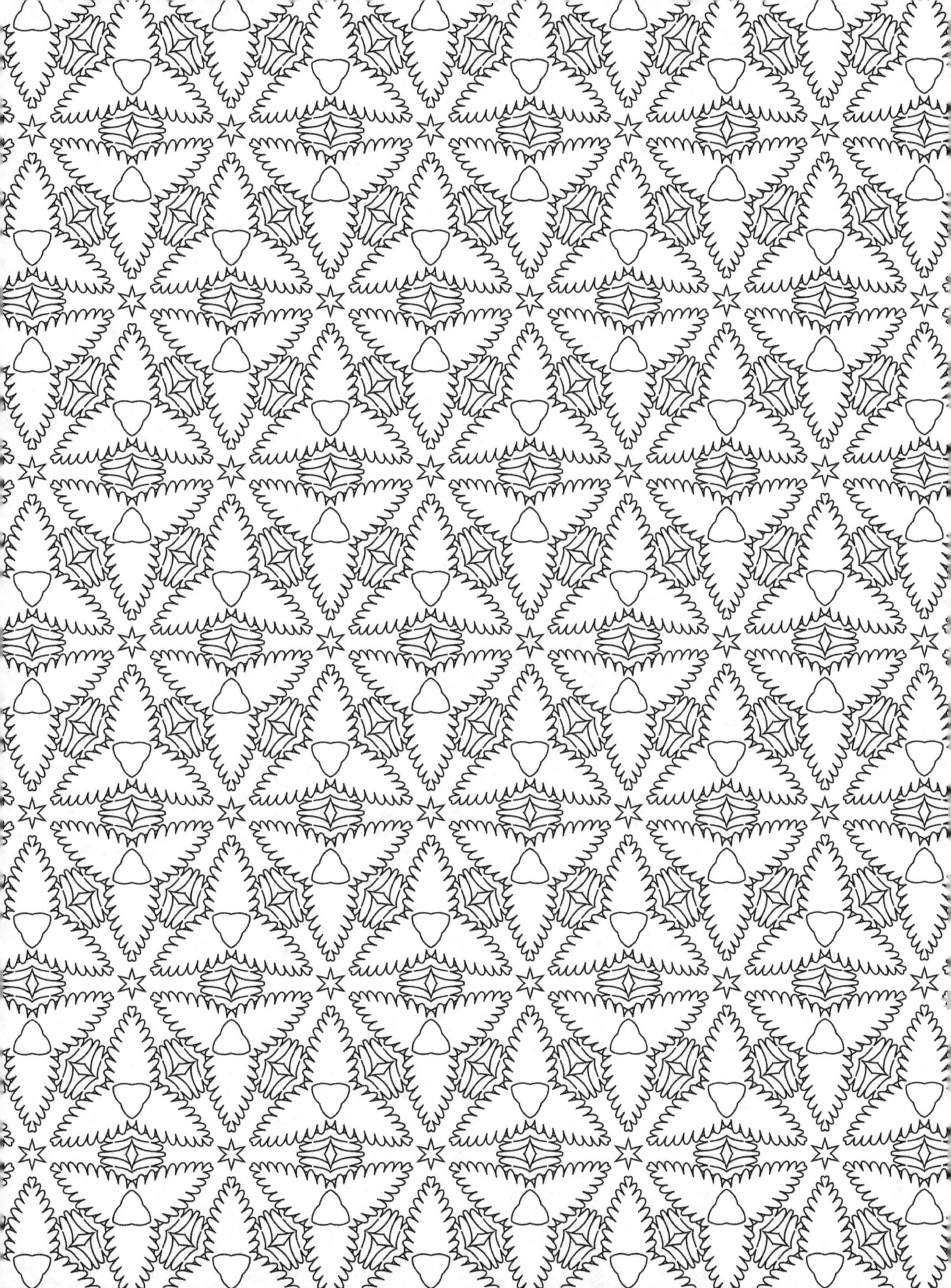

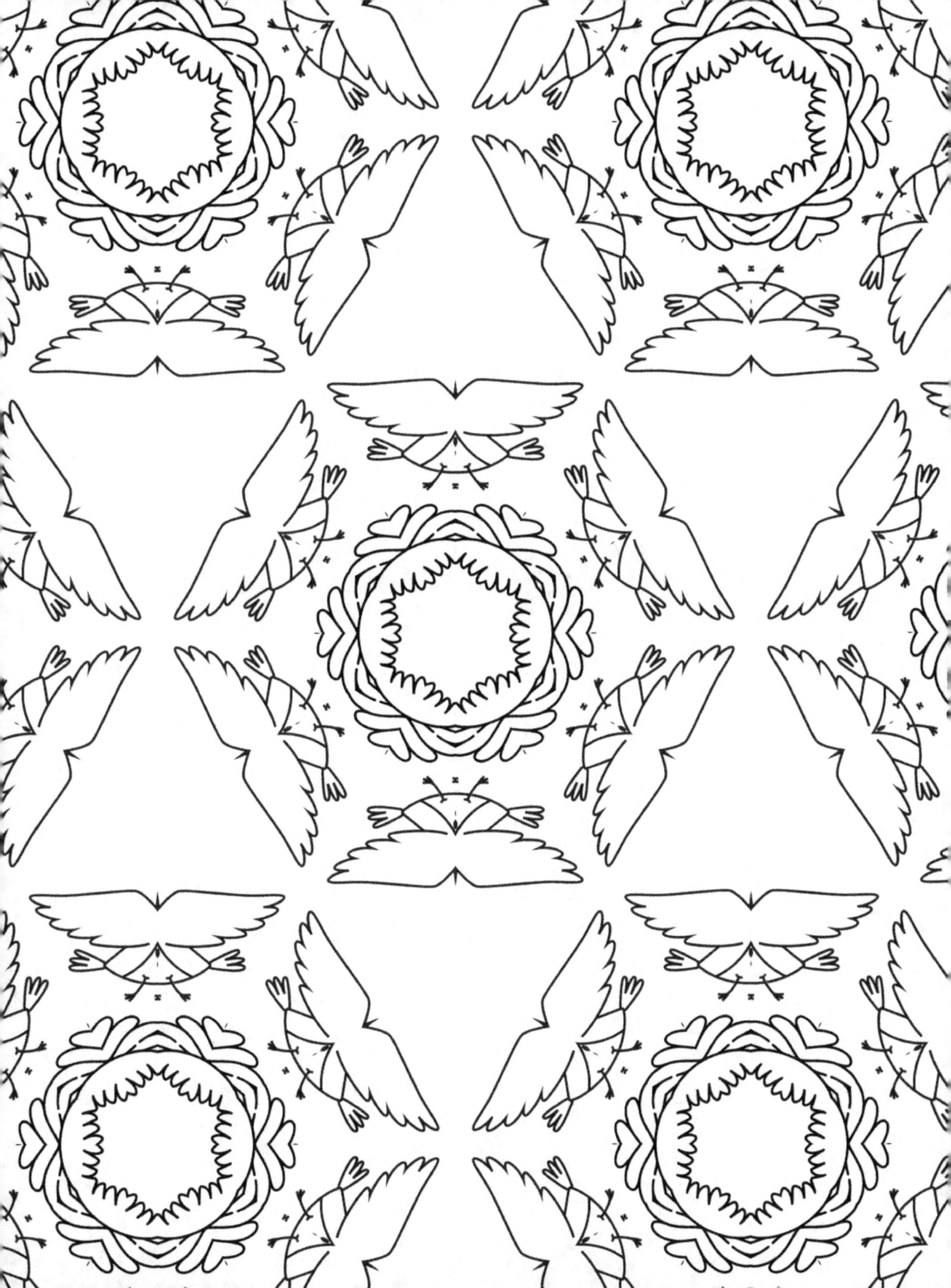

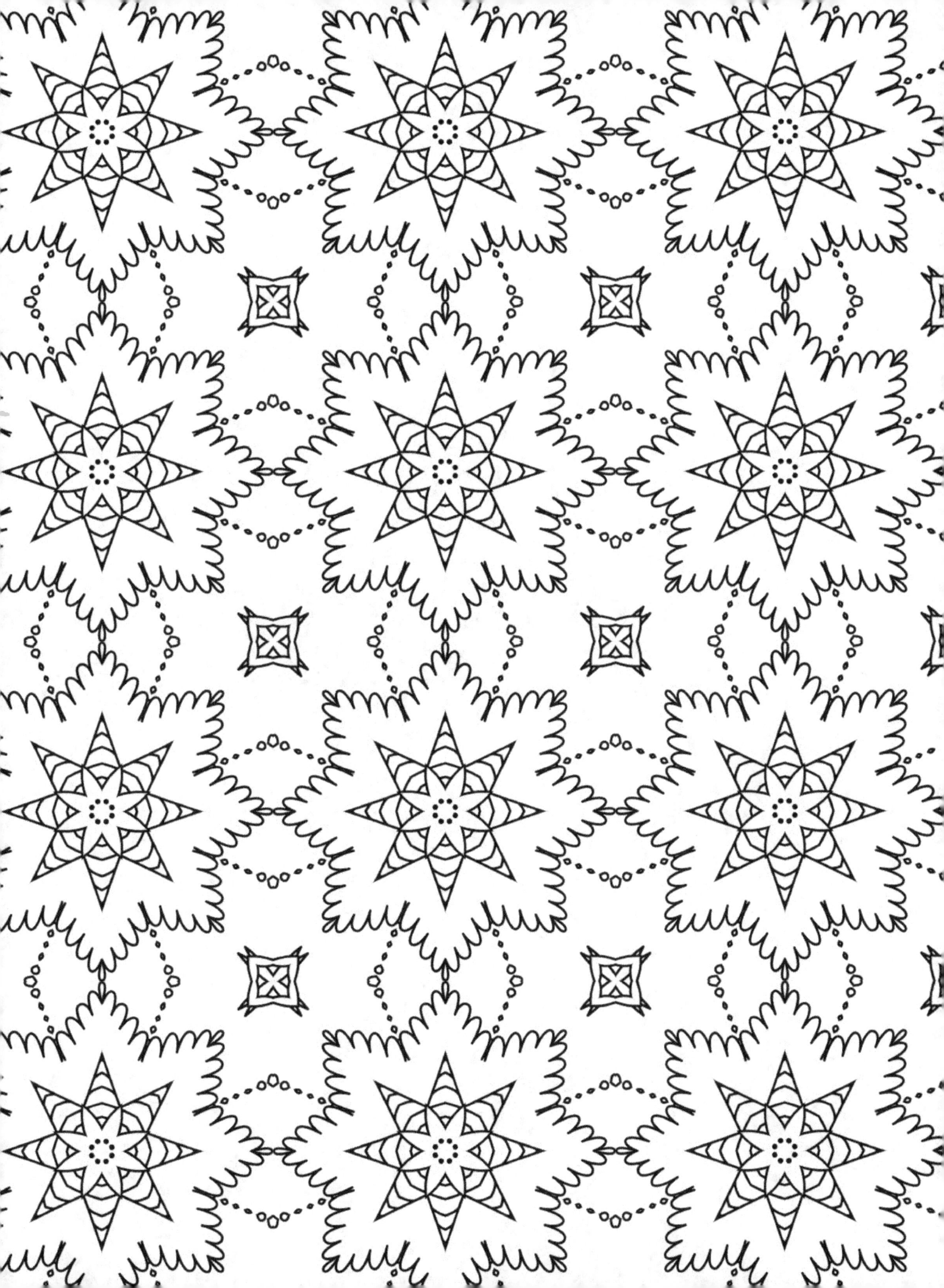

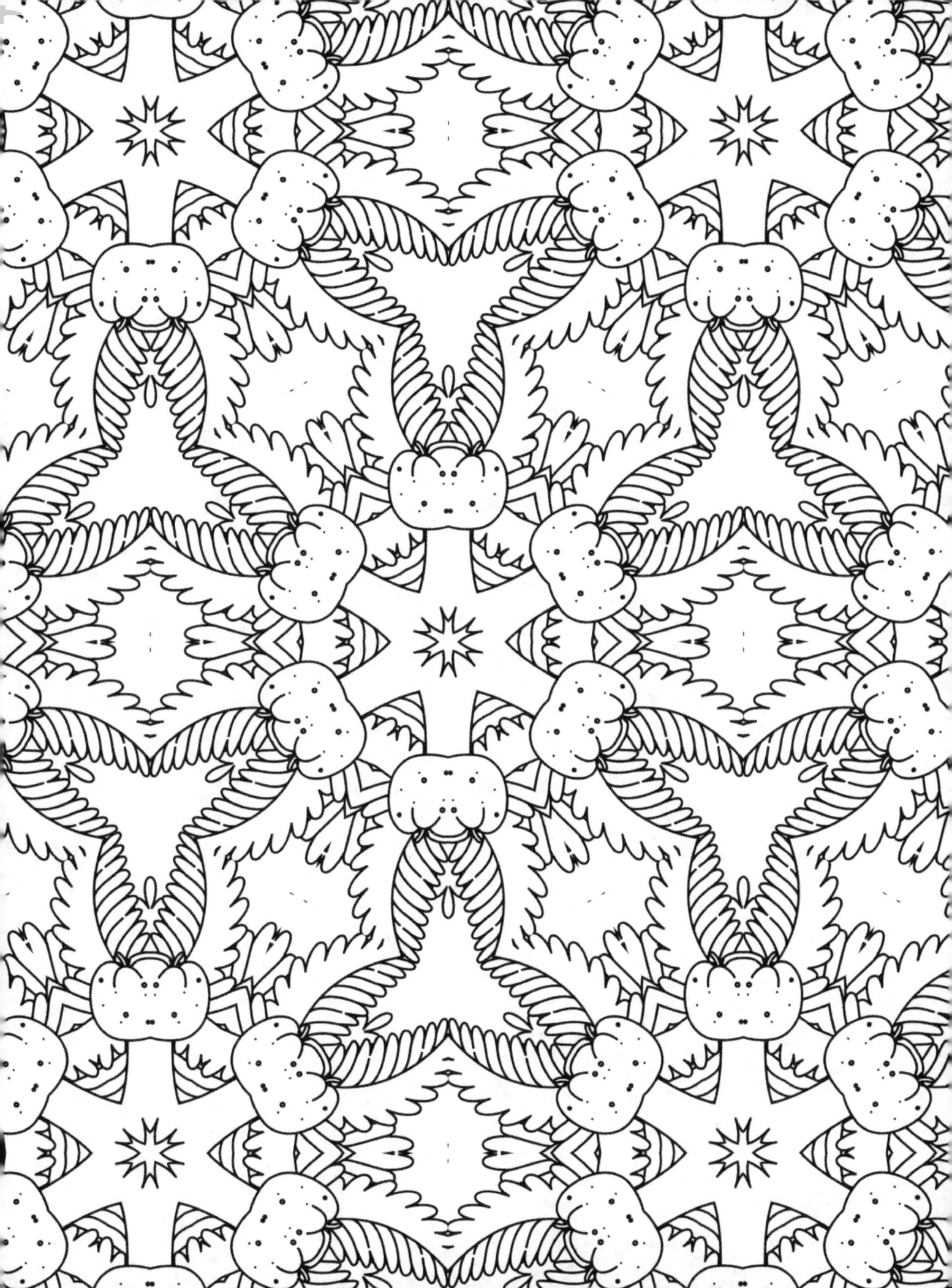

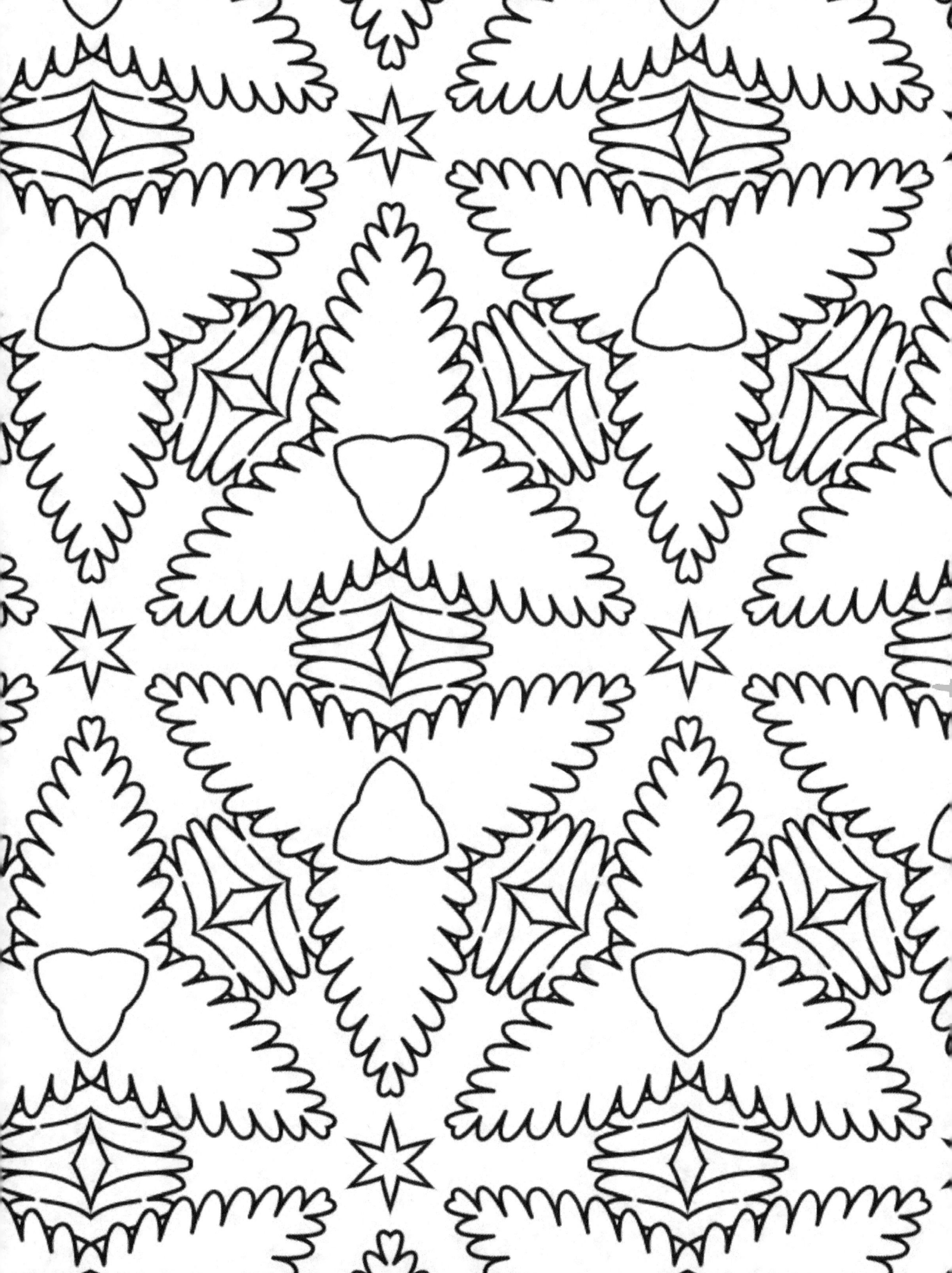

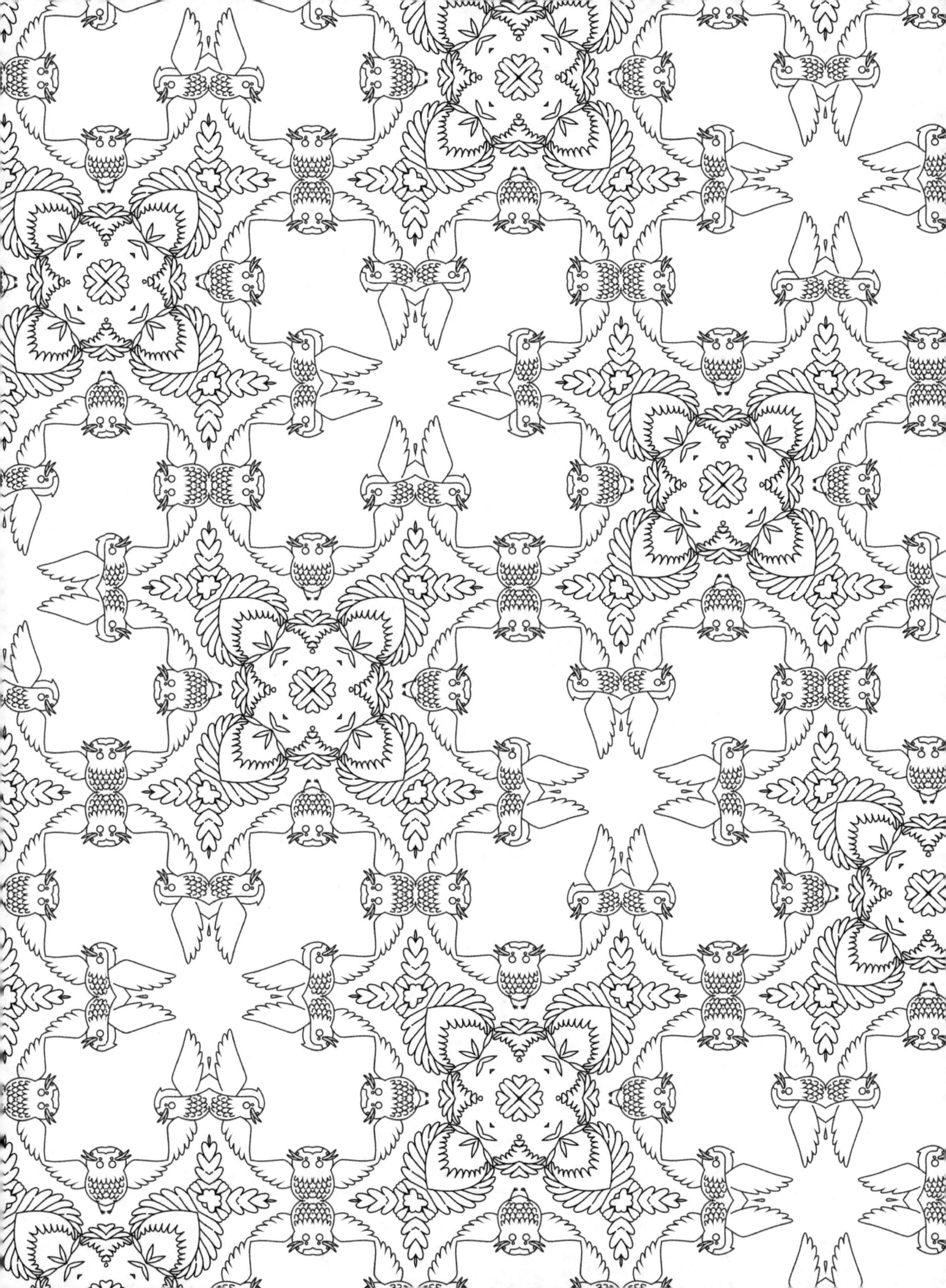

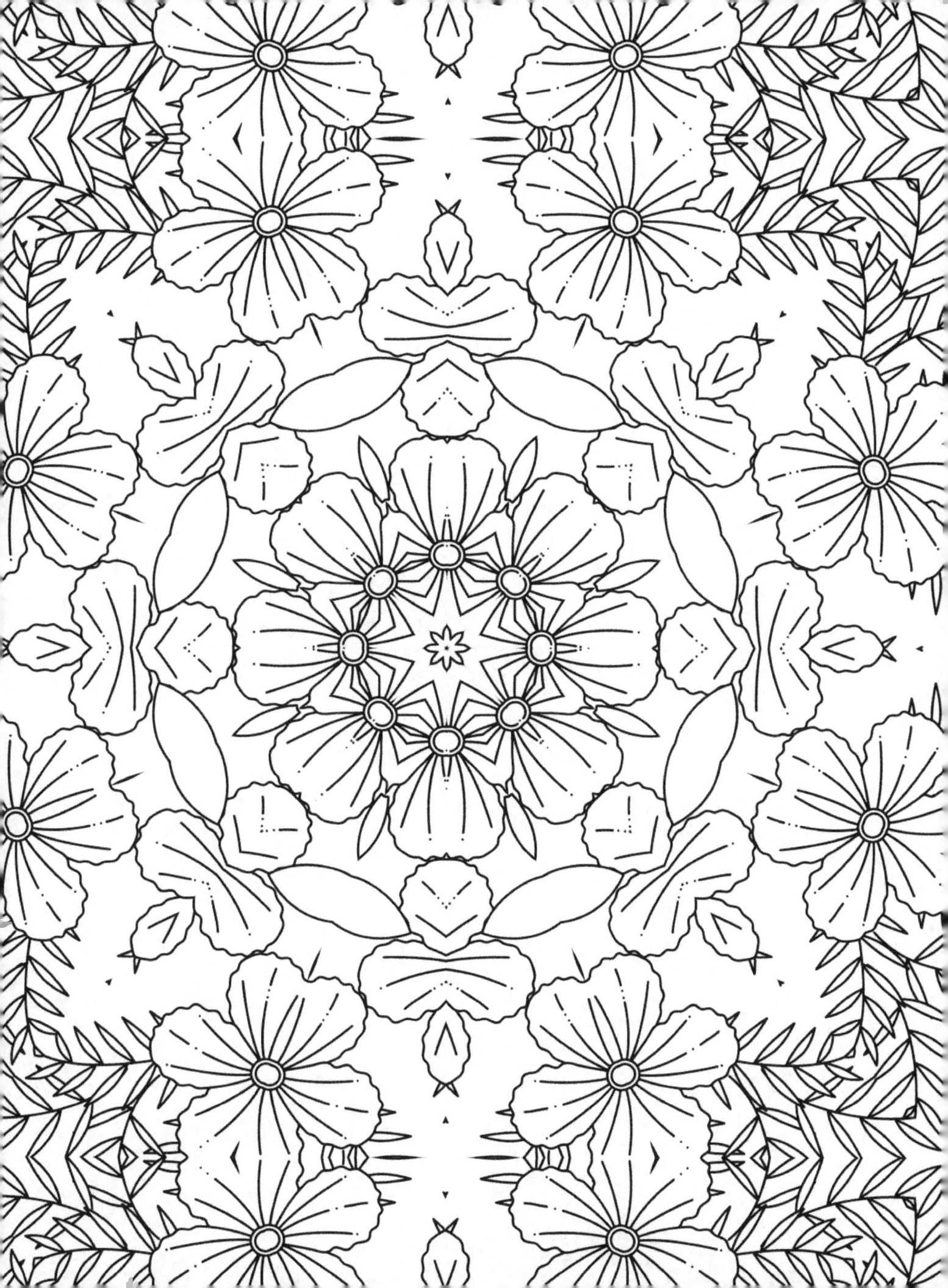

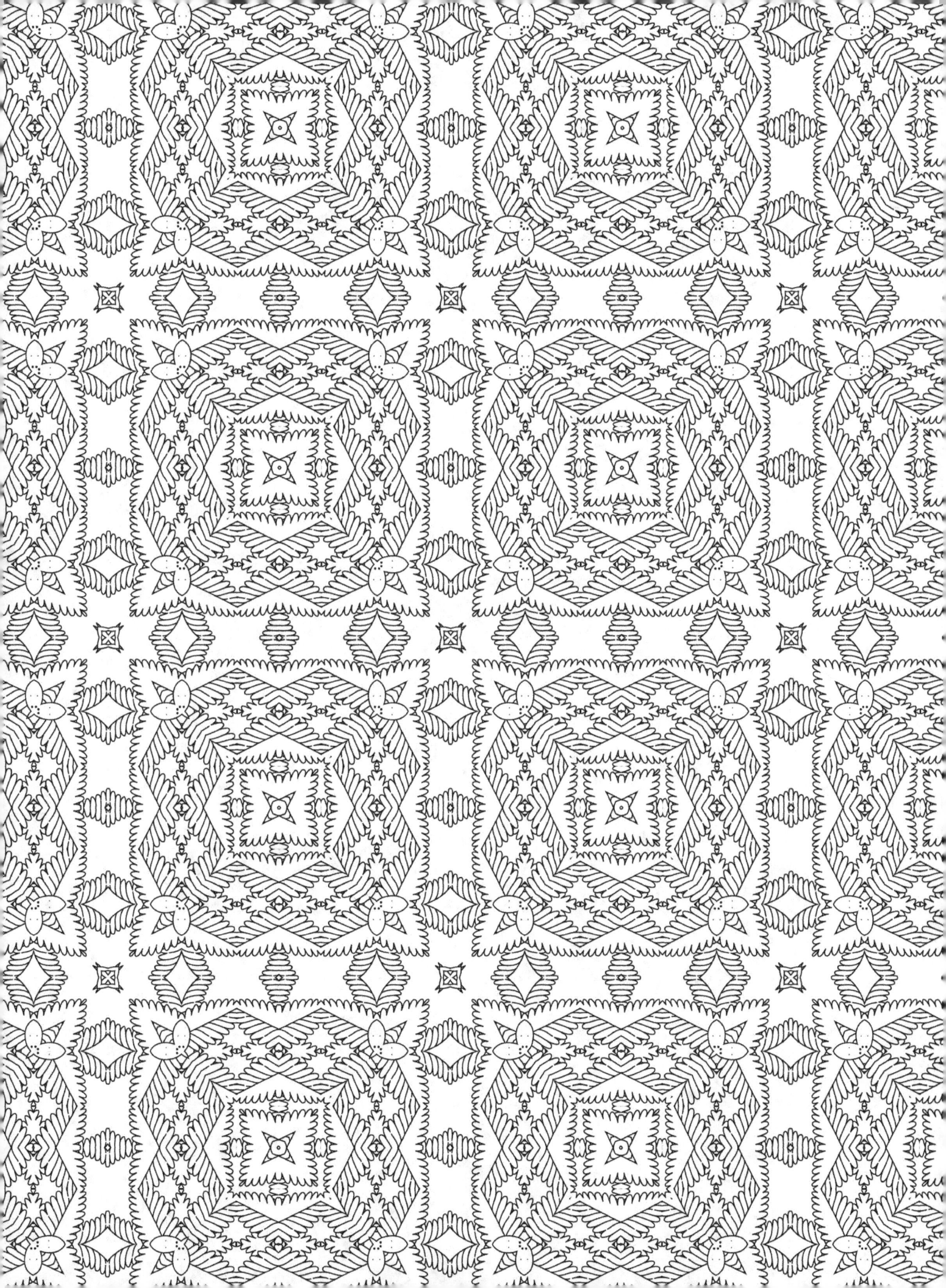

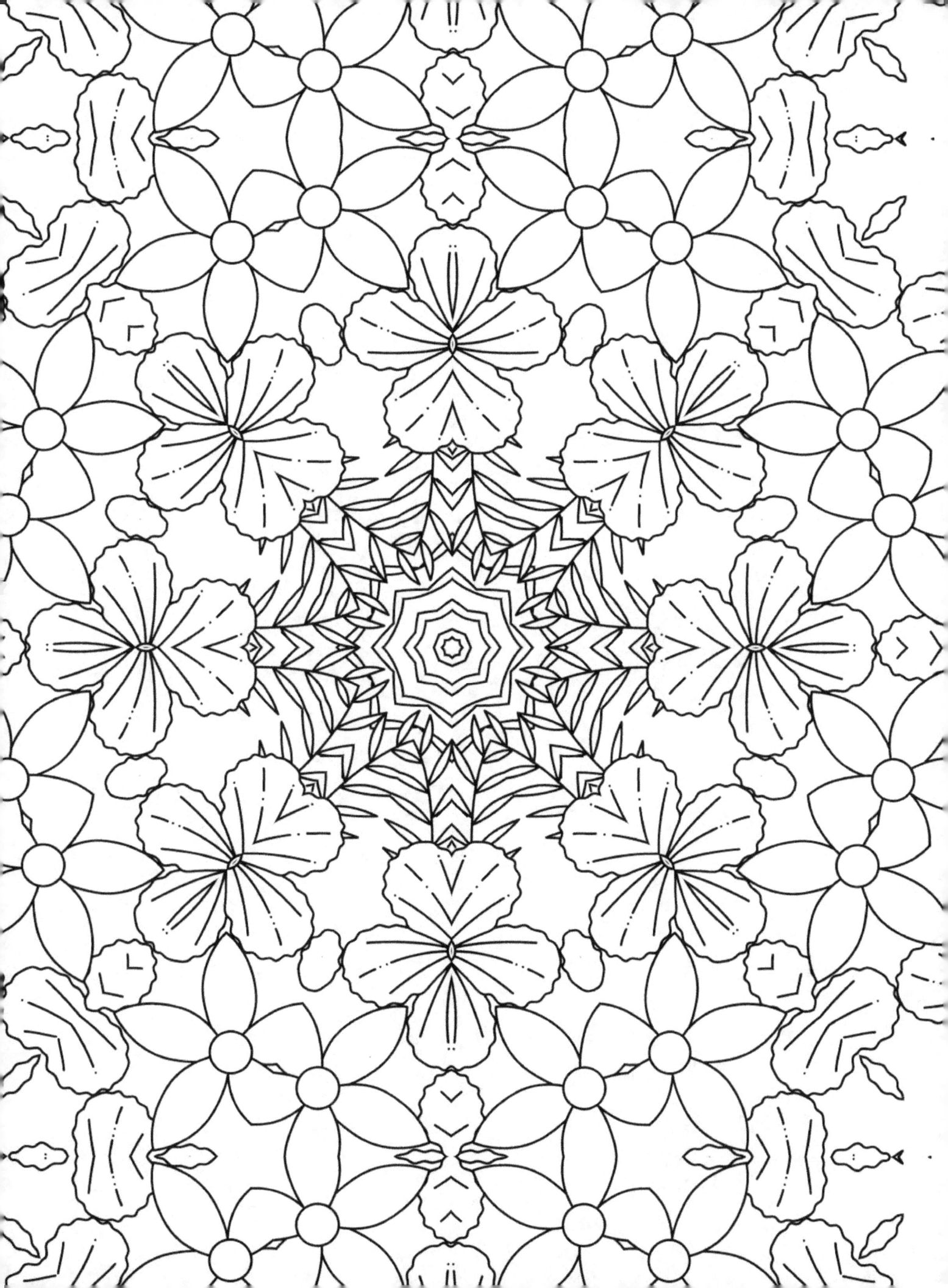

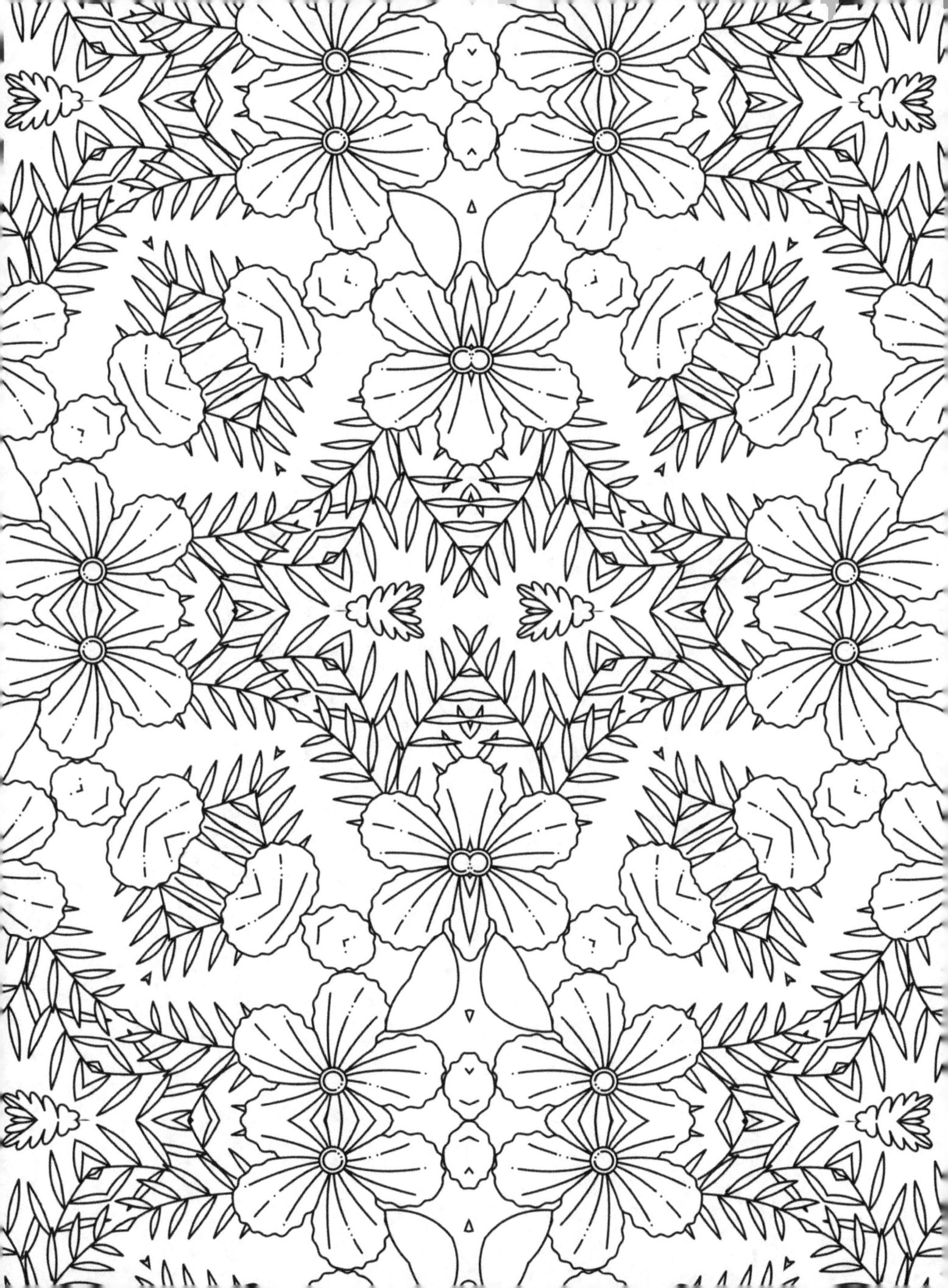

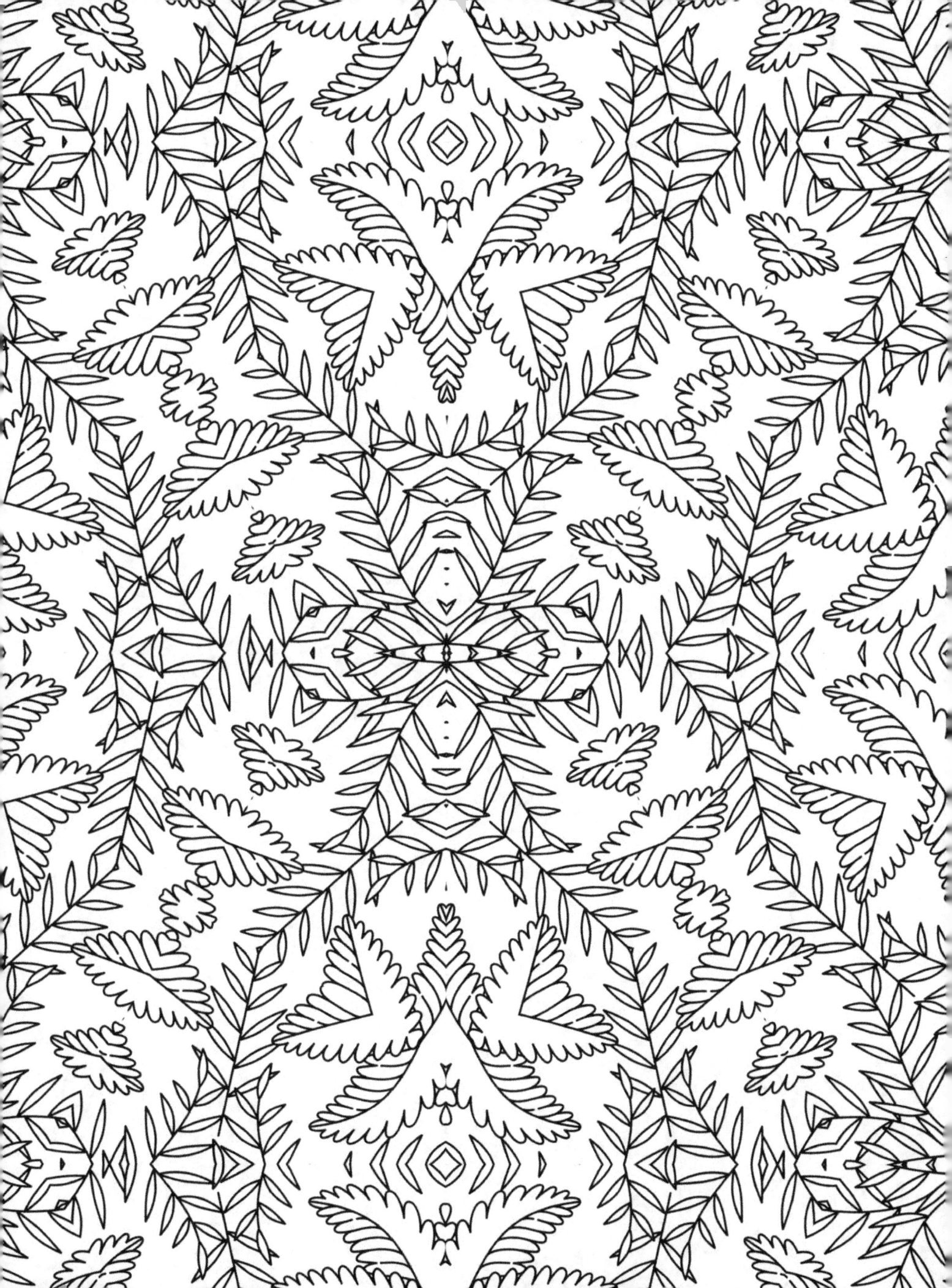

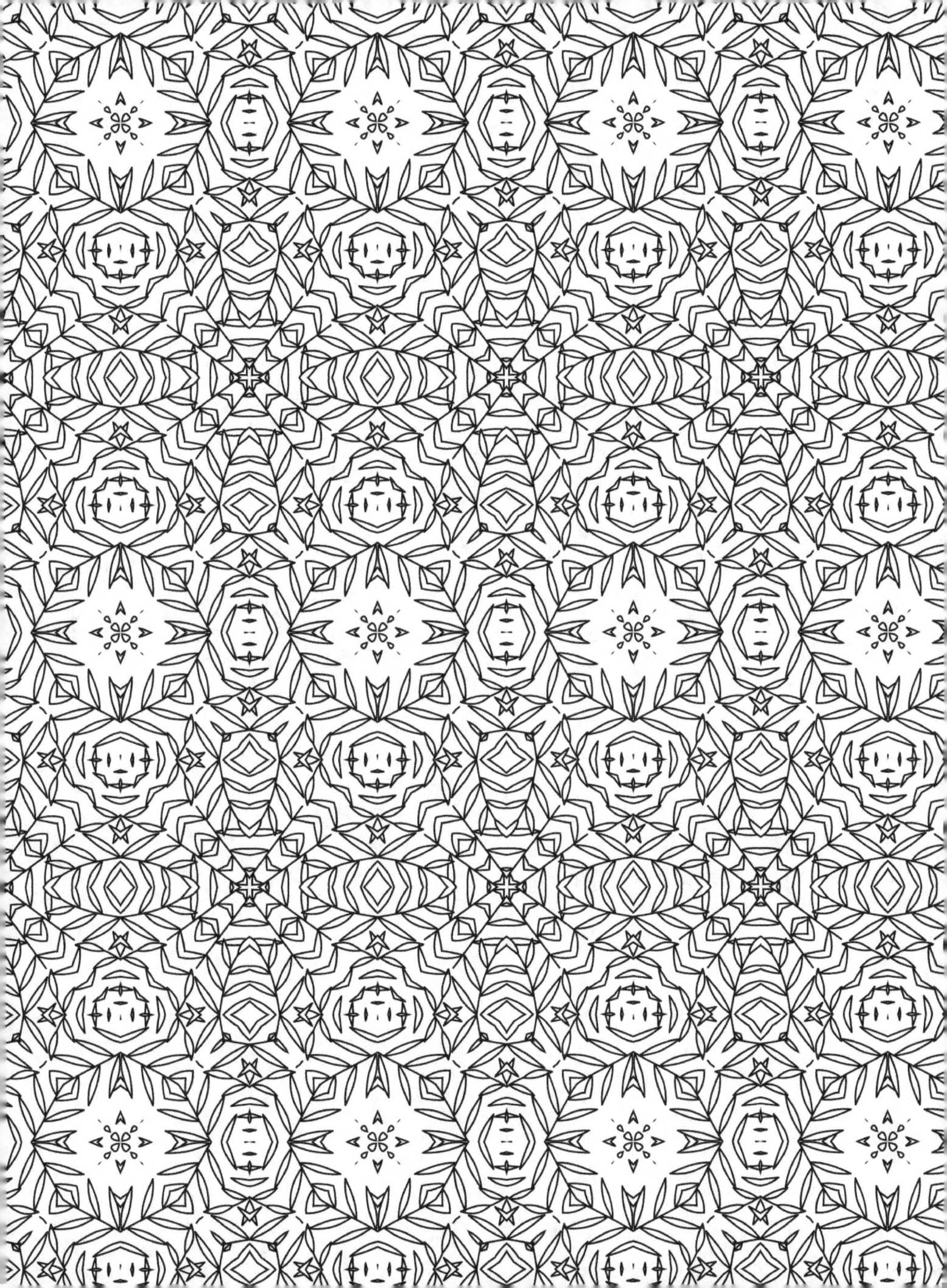

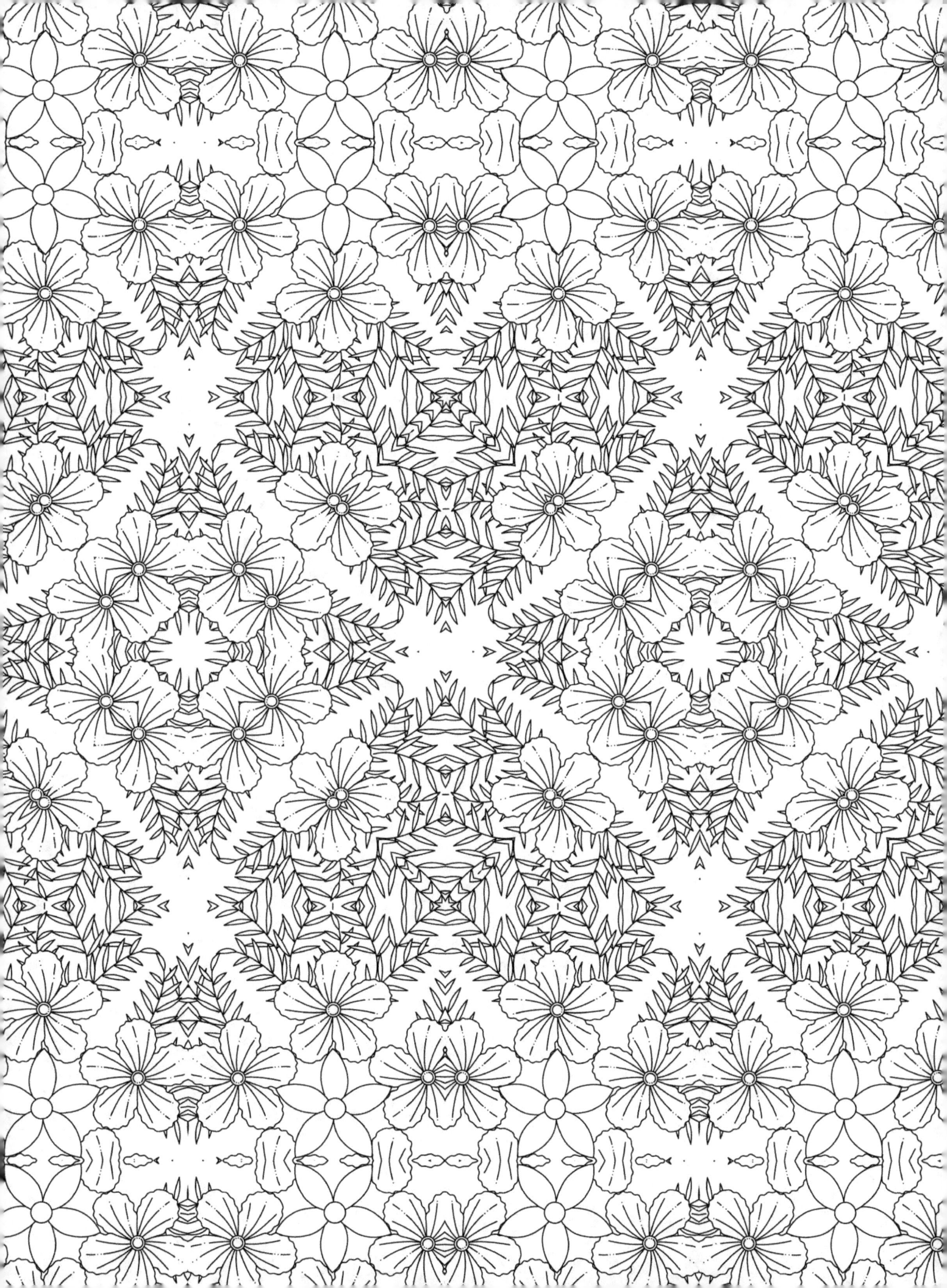

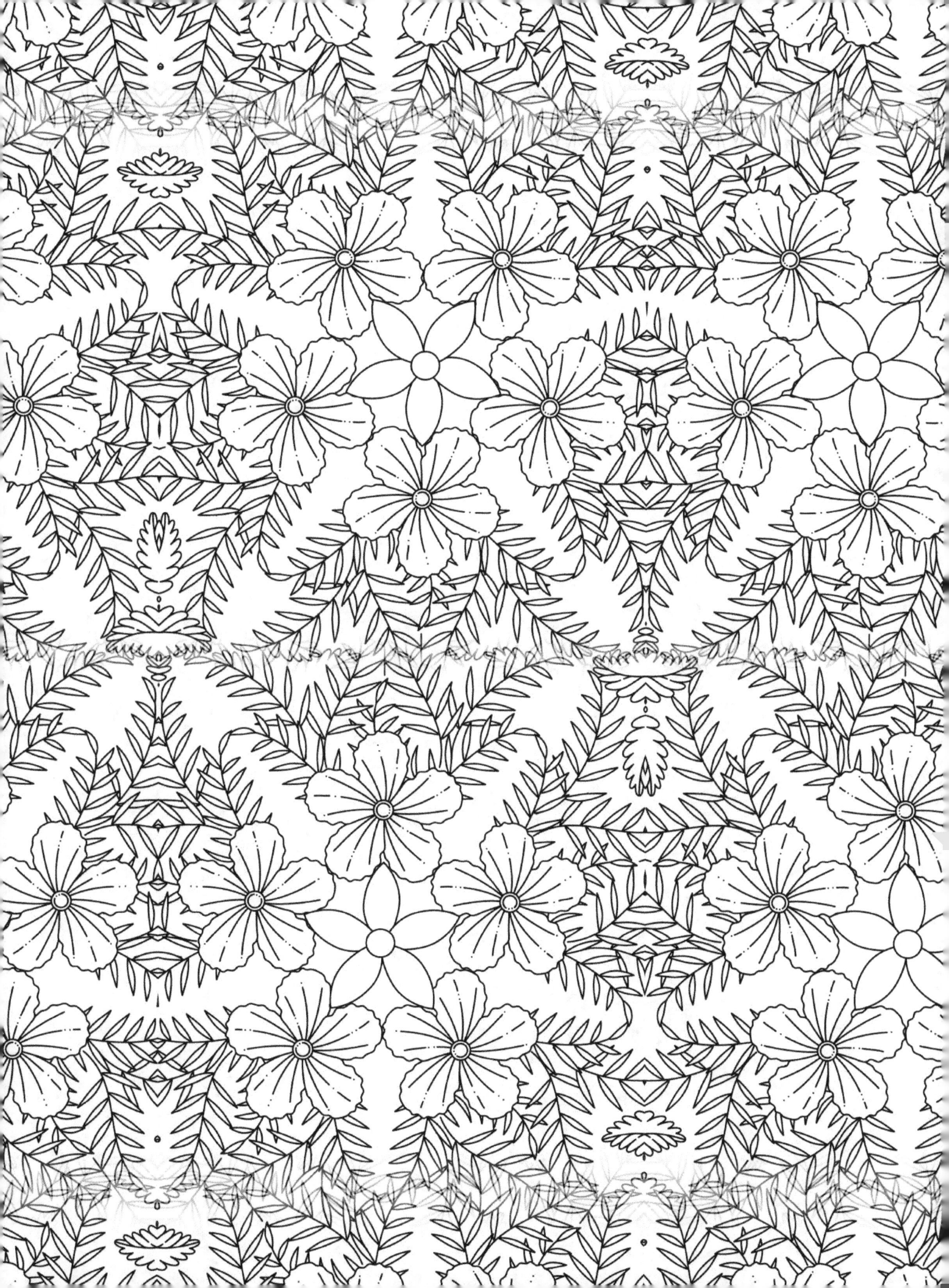

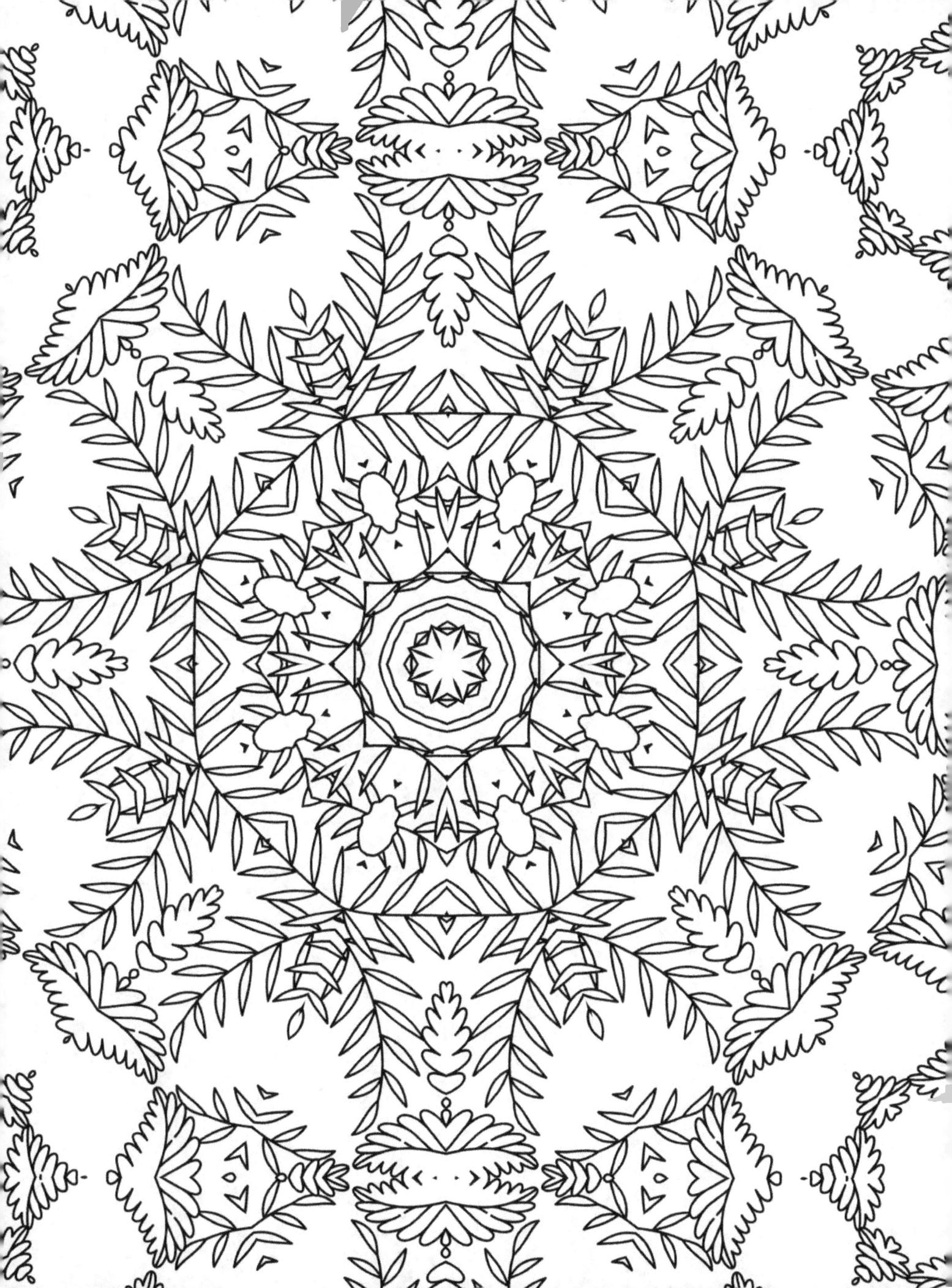

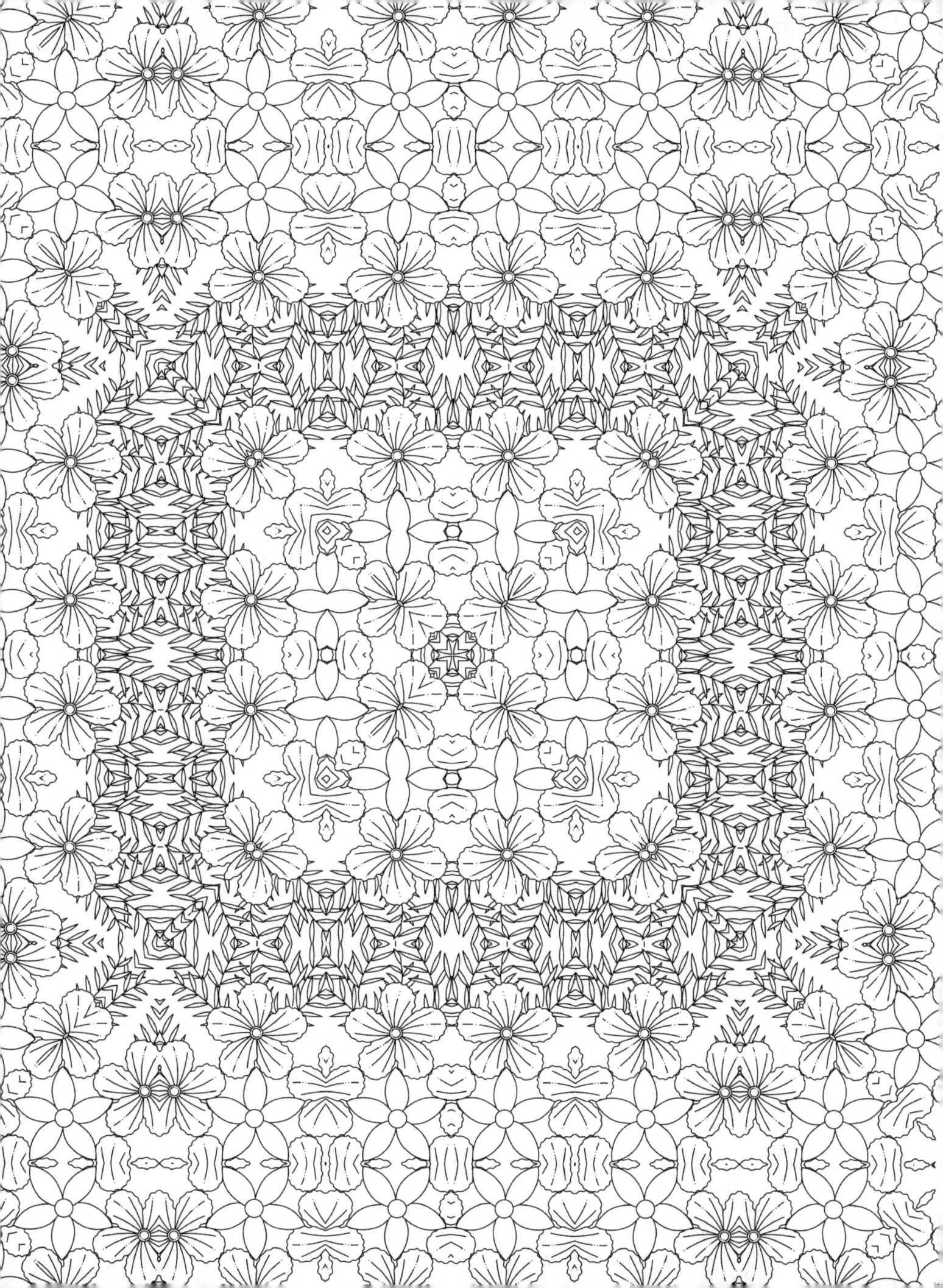

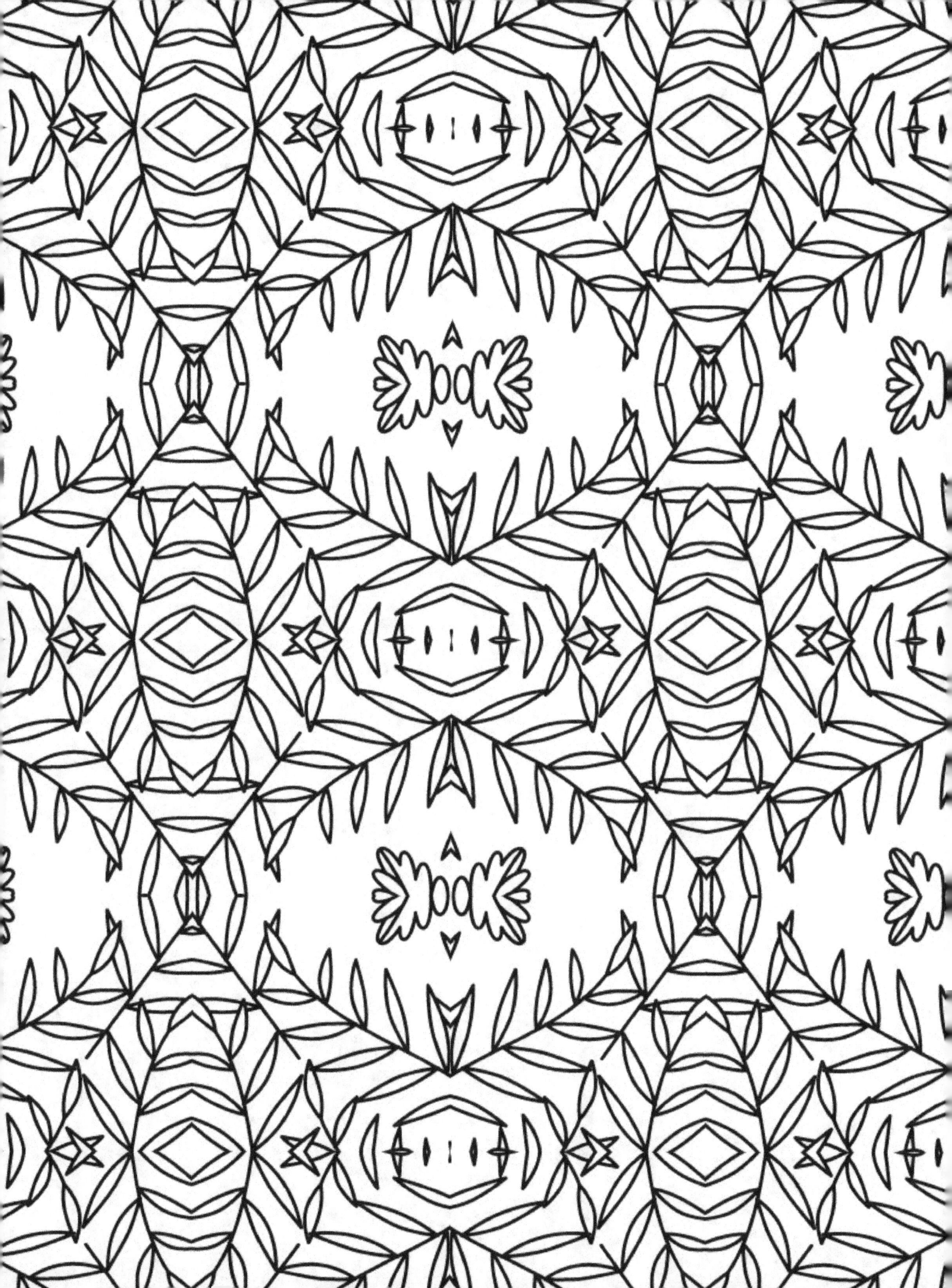

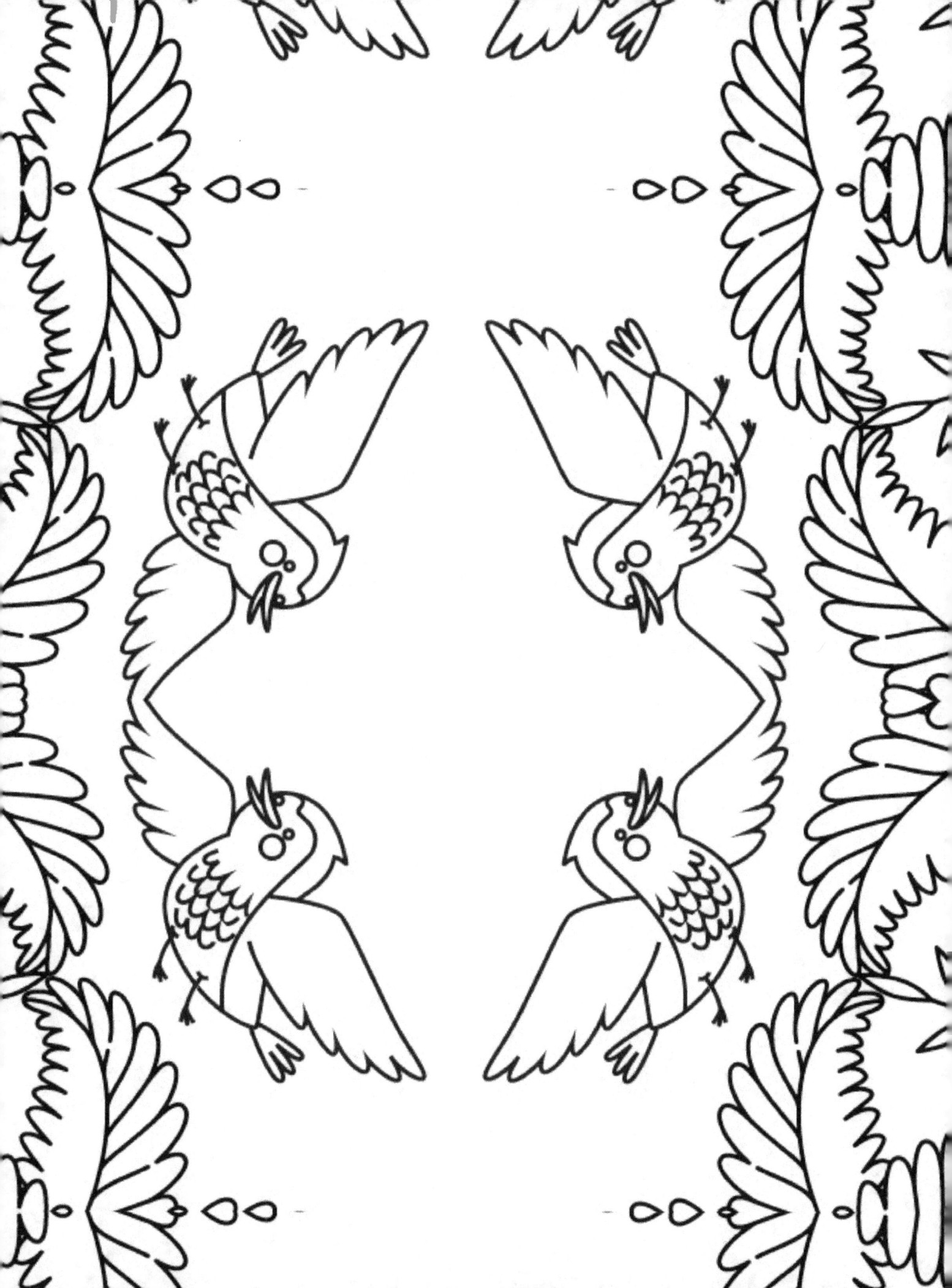

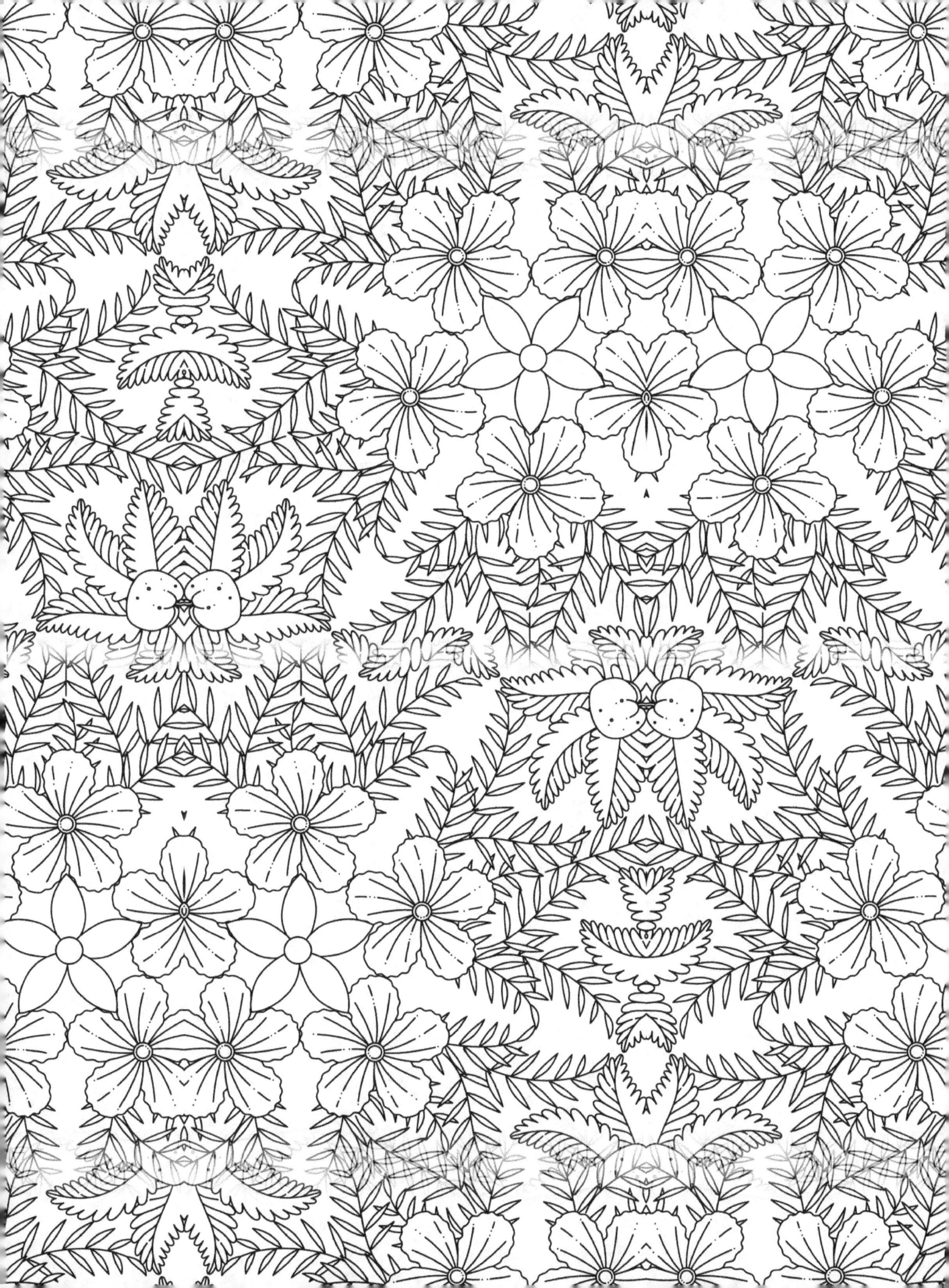

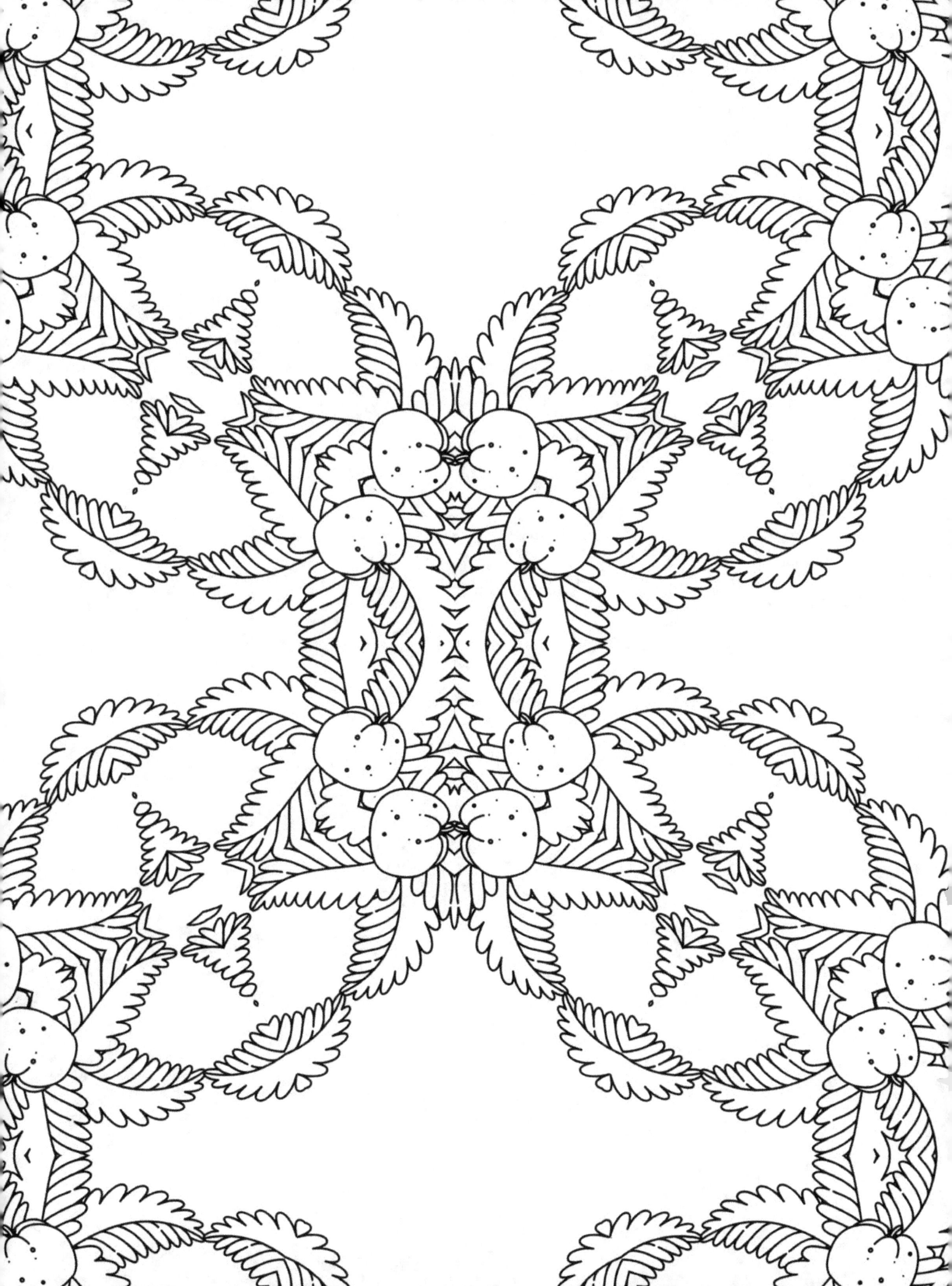

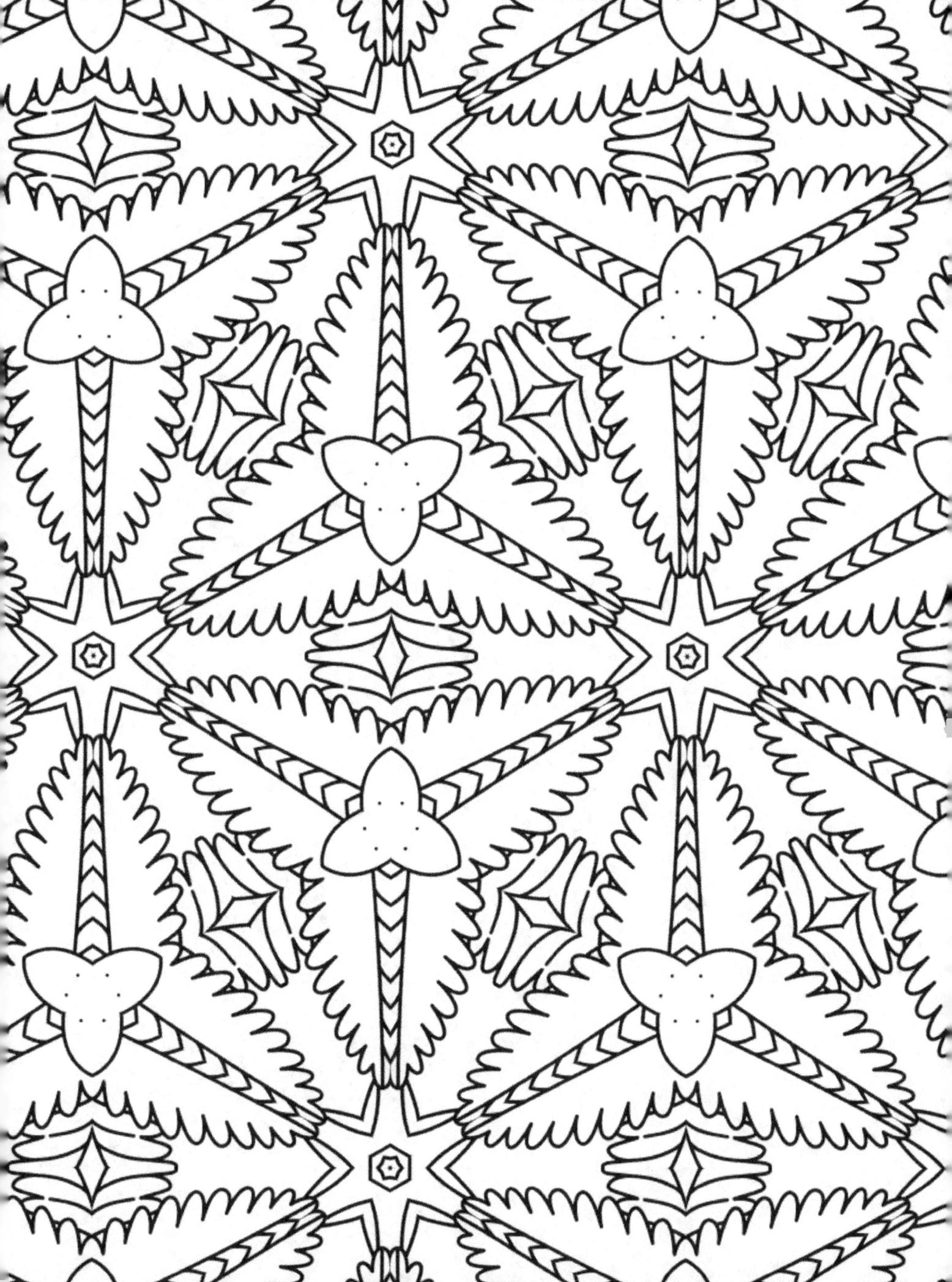

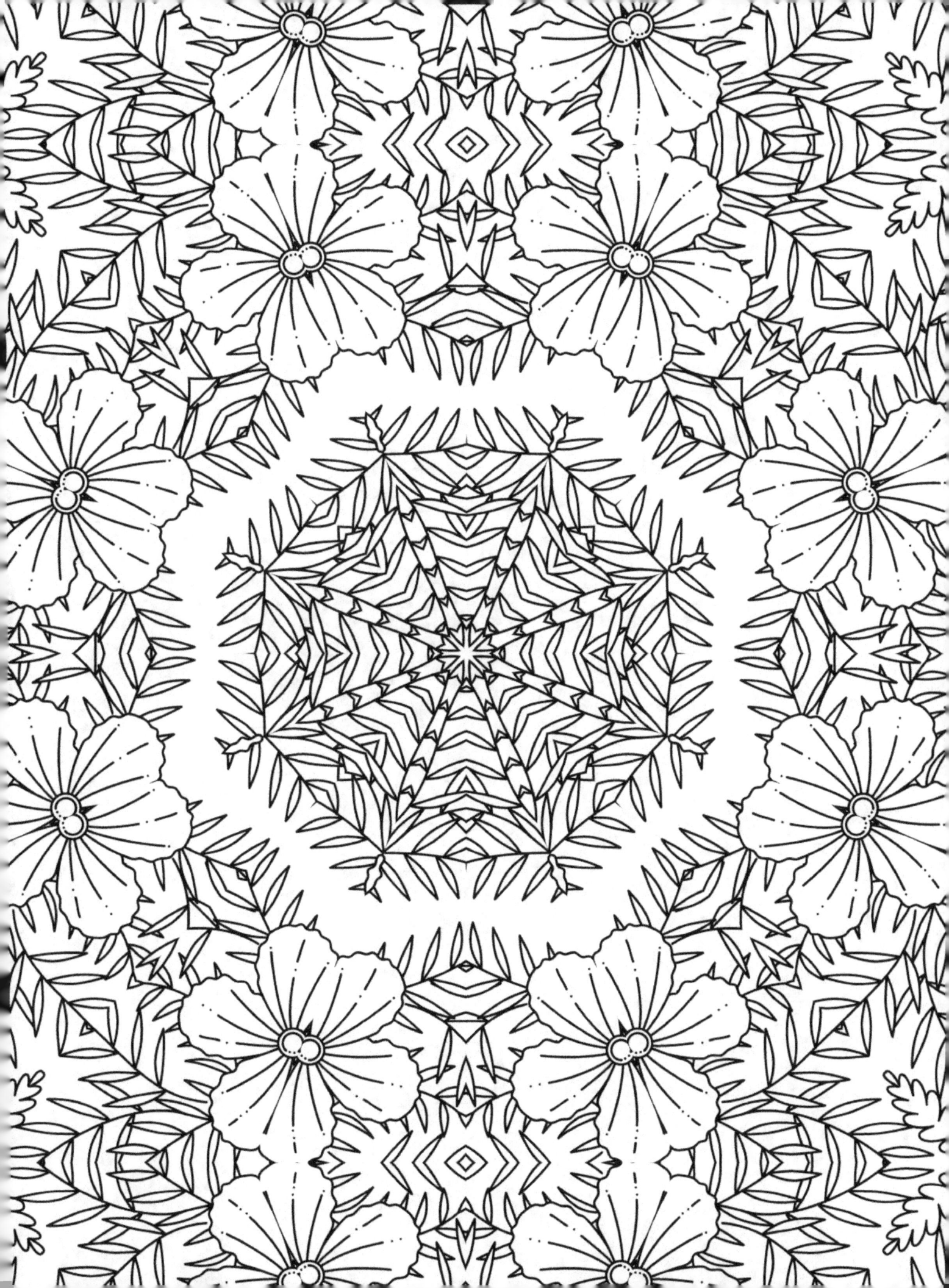

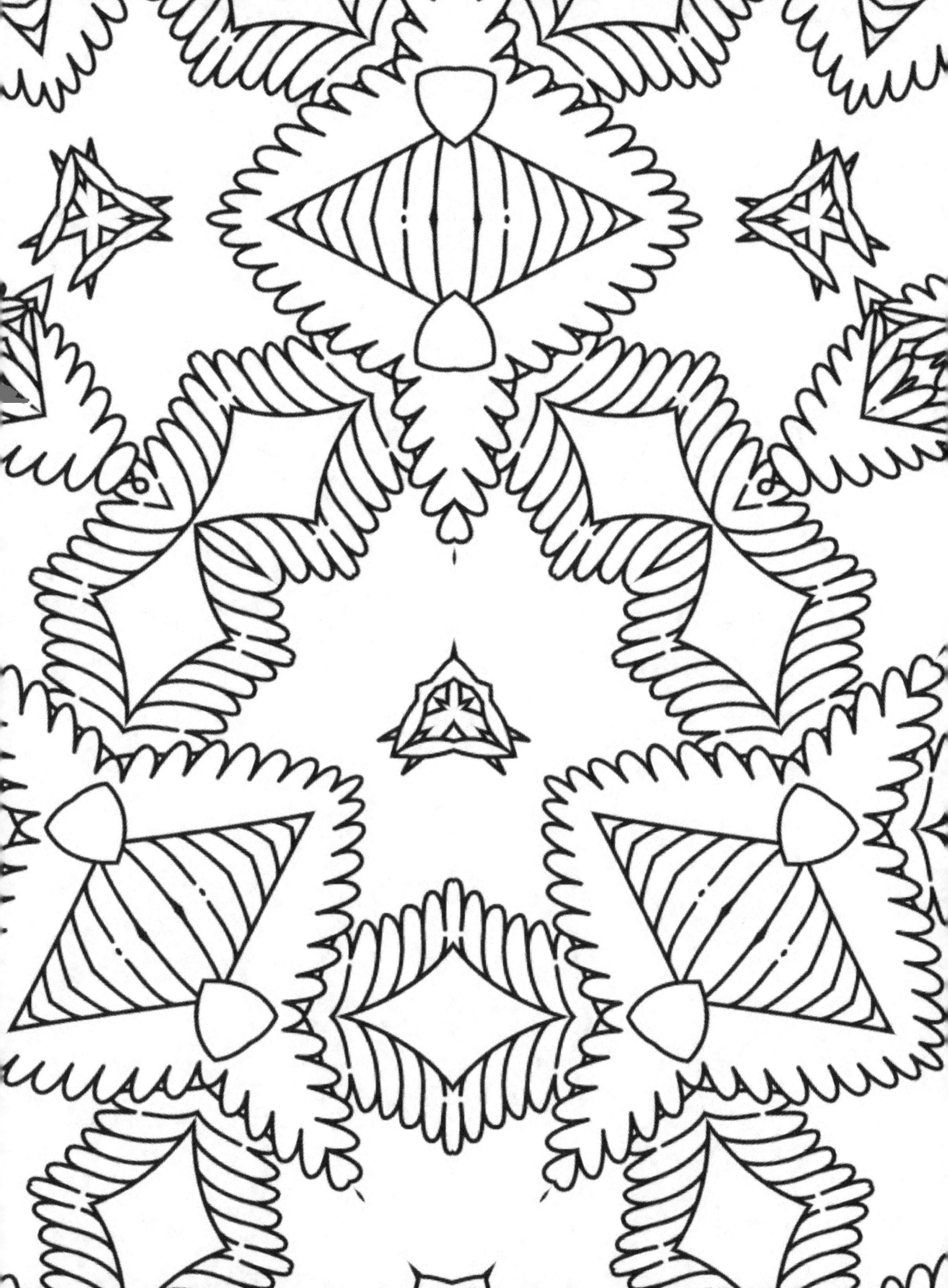

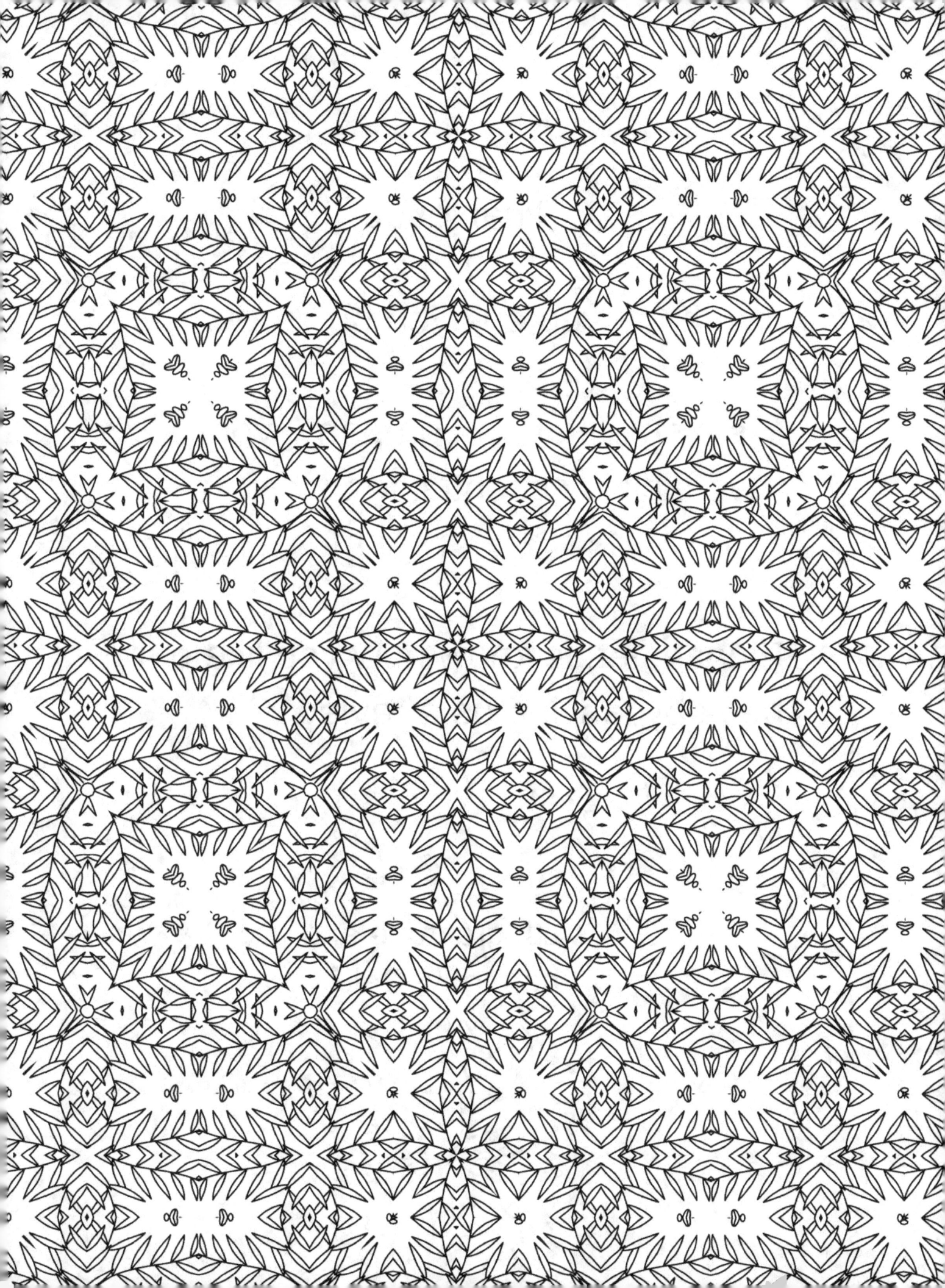

Thank you!

We hope you enjoyed our book.

As a small family company, your feedback is essential to us.

Please, let us know how you like our book by leaving us a review.

With gratitude and harmony, Dalu